OPPOSING VIEWPOINTS® SERIES

| Globalization

DATE DUE

Other Books of Related Interest:

Opposing Viewpoints Series

China

Human Rights

The United Nations

The World Trade Organization

Current Controversies Series

Capitalism

Fair Trade

The U.S. Economy

The World Economy

At Issue Series

Is the World Experiencing an Energy Crisis?

Is There a New Cold War?

Should the U.S. Close Its Borders?

What Is the Impact of Emigration?

"Congress shall make no law . . . abridging the freedom of speech, or of the press."

First Amendment to the U.S. Constitution

The basic foundation of our democracy is the First Amendment guarantee of freedom of expression. The Opposing Viewpoints Series is dedicated to the concept of this basic freedom and the idea that it is more important to practice it than to enshrine it.

Globalization

David Haugen and Rachael Mach, Book Editors

GREENHAVEN PRESS
A part of Gale, Cengage Learning

GALE
CENGAGE Learning™

Detroit • New York • San Francisco • New Haven, Conn • Waterville, Maine • London

Christine Nasso, *Publisher*
Elizabeth Des Chenes, *Managing Editor*

© 2010 Greenhaven Press, a part of Gale, Cengage Learning.

Gale and Greenhaven Press are registered trademarks used herein under license.

For more information, contact:
Greenhaven Press
27500 Drake Rd.
Farmington Hills, MI 48331-3535
Or you can visit our Internet site at gale.cengage.com

For product information and technology assistance, contact us at

Gale Customer Support, 1-800-877-4253
For permission to use material from this text or product, submit all requests online at
www.cengage.com/permissions

Further permissions questions can be emailed to permissionrequest@cengage.com

Articles in Greenhaven Press anthologies are often edited for length to meet page requirements. In addition, original titles of these works are changed to clearly present the main thesis and to explicitly indicate the author's opinion. Every effort is made to ensure that Greenhaven Press accurately reflects the original intent of the authors. Every effort has been made to trace the owners of copyrighted material.

Cover photograph © John Foxx/Stockbyte/Getty Images.

LIBRARY OF CONGRESS CATALOGING-IN-PUBLICATION DATA

Globalization / David Haugen and Rachael Mach, book editors.
 p. cm. -- (Opposing viewpoints)
 Includes bibliographical references and index.
 ISBN 978-0-7377-4771-3 (hardcover) -- ISBN 978-0-7377-4772-0 (pbk.)
 1. 1. Globalization--Juvenile literature. I. I. Haugen, David M., 1969- II. Mach, Rachael.
 JZ1318.G5786223 2010
 303.48'2--dc22
                                                              2009041735

Printed in the United States of America
1 2 3 4 5 6 7 14 13 12 11 10

Contents

Chapter 3: How Does Globalization Affect Developing Nations?

Chapter 4: How Is Globalization Impacting the U.S. Economy?

Why Consider Opposing Viewpoints?

> *"The only way in which a human being can make some approach to knowing the whole of a subject is by hearing what can be said about it by persons of every variety of opinion and studying all modes in which it can be looked at by every character of mind. No wise man ever acquired his wisdom in any mode but this."*
>
> John Stuart Mill

In our media-intensive culture it is not difficult to find differing opinions. Thousands of newspapers and magazines and dozens of radio and television talk shows resound with differing points of view. The difficulty lies in deciding which opinion to agree with and which "experts" seem the most credible. The more inundated we become with differing opinions and claims, the more essential it is to hone critical reading and thinking skills to evaluate these ideas. Opposing Viewpoints books address this problem directly by presenting stimulating debates that can be used to enhance and teach these skills. The varied opinions contained in each book examine many different aspects of a single issue. While examining these conveniently edited opposing views, readers can develop critical thinking skills such as the ability to compare and contrast authors' credibility, facts, argumentation styles, use of persuasive techniques, and other stylistic tools. In short, the Opposing Viewpoints Series is an ideal way to attain the higher-level thinking and reading skills so essential in a culture of diverse and contradictory opinions.

In addition to providing a tool for critical thinking, Opposing Viewpoints books challenge readers to question their own strongly held opinions and assumptions. Most people form their opinions on the basis of upbringing, peer pressure, and personal, cultural, or professional bias. By reading carefully balanced opposing views, readers must directly confront new ideas as well as the opinions of those with whom they disagree. This is not to simplistically argue that everyone who reads opposing views will—or should—change his or her opinion. Instead, the series enhances readers' understanding of their own views by encouraging confrontation with opposing ideas. Careful examination of others' views can lead to the readers' understanding of the logical inconsistencies in their own opinions, perspective on why they hold an opinion, and the consideration of the possibility that their opinion requires further evaluation.

Evaluating Other Opinions

To ensure that this type of examination occurs, Opposing Viewpoints books present all types of opinions. Prominent spokespeople on different sides of each issue as well as well-known professionals from many disciplines challenge the reader. An additional goal of the series is to provide a forum for other, less known, or even unpopular viewpoints. The opinion of an ordinary person who has had to make the decision to cut off life support from a terminally ill relative, for example, may be just as valuable and provide just as much insight as a medical ethicist's professional opinion. The editors have two additional purposes in including these less known views. One, the editors encourage readers to respect others' opinions—even when not enhanced by professional credibility. It is only by reading or listening to and objectively evaluating others' ideas that one can determine whether they are worthy of consideration. Two, the inclusion of such viewpoints encourages the important critical thinking skill of objectively evaluating an author's credentials and bias. This evaluation will illuminate an author's reasons for taking a particular stance on an issue and will aid in readers' evaluation of the author's ideas.

It is our hope that these books will give readers a deeper understanding of the issues debated and an appreciation of the complexity of even seemingly simple issues when good and honest people disagree. This awareness is particularly important in a democratic society such as ours in which people enter into public debate to determine the common good. Those with whom one disagrees should not be regarded as enemies but rather as people whose views deserve careful examination and may shed light on one's own.

Thomas Jefferson once said that "difference of opinion leads to inquiry, and inquiry to truth." Jefferson, a broadly educated man, argued that "if a nation expects to be ignorant and free . . . it expects what never was and never will be." As individuals and as a nation, it is imperative that we consider the opinions of others and examine them with skill and discernment. The Opposing Viewpoints Series is intended to help readers achieve this goal.

David L. Bender and Bruno Leone,
Founders

Introduction

> *"Globalization has enabled individuals, corporations and nation-states to influence actions and events around the world—faster, deeper and cheaper than ever before—and equally to derive benefits for them. Globalization has led to the opening, the vanishing of many barriers and walls, and has the potential for expanding freedom, democracy, innovation, social and cultural exchanges while offering outstanding opportunities for dialogue and understanding."*
>
> *—Pascal Lamy,*
> *director-general of the World*
> *Trade Organization, January 30, 2006*

> *"The benefits of globalization need to be spread more widely. Maximizing these benefits, ensuring that more people gain, and harnessing technology and economic integration to help meet poverty reduction goals are among the most critical challenges we face today. Something else that is clear is that the problems of tomorrow are likely to be truly global. Their solutions need to be global, too."*
>
> *—Saleh M. Nsouli,*
> *director of European offices of the*
> *International Monetary Fund,*
> *July 25, 2008*

Although international and intercontinental trade has occurred for centuries, only since the 1980s has the term *globalization* been widely used to denote the modern flow of capital from one nation to another. The rise of the term specifically accompanied the growth of technological innovations—most significantly the Internet—that made the scheduling and recording of international shipments as well as the transfer of payments quicker and easier. As rapid communication networks brought far-flung businesses together, so, too, did the new technology bring disparate cultures together, expanding the concept of globalization to include the spread of ideas, media, the arts, politics, and other social artifacts across the planet. Thus today globalization has evolved beyond its economic roots to refer to all forces that connect peoples and societies and shrink the distances between them.

Whether the expansion of markets and the commingling of cultures is desired by or even beneficial to all involved is a matter of great debate. Advocates of free trade insist that facilitating business and communication between countries brings people together and provides opportunities for increased prosperity. Globalization's critics worry that globalization is often one-sided, endowing Western multinational companies with a means of exploiting developing nations and imposing business models, products, and even values on people who often do not welcome the intrusion.

Within this debate, the economic aspects of globalization clearly dominate current discussions. On the supply side of the economic chain, globalization entails the division of labor on a global scale. Corporations can outsource the manufacture of products to firms in foreign lands; in fact, advocates of globalization claim that almost every part of a business—including product design, testing, marketing, manufacture, and customer service—can be doled out to foreign companies that can do the best work at the cheapest price. This allows a computer company in the United States, for example, to tap into the skilled technician teams in India as well as the pool of unskilled assembly workers in China to bring a finished product to market. And, as supporters would argue, because the computer company will seek the best quality at the lowest cost when outsourcing, its product will be competitively priced for consumers.

Outsourcing also allows companies to refrain from making huge investments in infrastructure and personnel. Globalization's proponents contend that businesses can conserve funds and simply take advantage of outsourcing when needed. Outsourcing even typically provides corporations with market outlets in the countries where they have part of their work done. According to the Specialty Graphic Imaging Association, "Offshore locations [will] develop into strong markets for U.S. products. Global markets with the purchasing power to buy U.S. products, coupled with increased near-source manufacturing, will benefit U.S. businesses."

Pro-globalization organizations also emphasize what they see as free trade's benefits to consumers. As mentioned, globalization tends to reduce the overall price for goods and services, and as more companies take advantage of global production chains, competition will supposedly make goods even more affordable. By spreading affordable products throughout many countries—especially developing countries—globalization ideally gives citizens in each country the opportunity to buy items or services that may otherwise have been unavailable. Globalization's advocates argue that this promotes more choice for consumers and raises their purchasing power as competitive markets keep prices at their lowest. They maintain that globalization raises the standard of living in countries where outsourcing is employing large numbers of people, and these workers, in turn, become consumers who are more easily able to purchase necessities and even luxury goods. As the World Bank has noted, more than 400 million Chinese have escaped poverty between 1990 and 2004 chiefly because of the rapidly globalized economy that is utilizing China's huge labor pool. And economic policies in China are now permitting more imports to reach consumers' hands so that China's middle class is growing.

Advocates of free trade also contend that the factors responsible for economic growth tend to influence other aspects of society as well. The International Monetary Fund concluded in a 2008 briefing:

> The broad reach of globalization easily extends to daily choices of personal, economic, and political life. For example, greater access to modern technologies, in the world of health care, could make the difference between life and death. In the world of communications, it would facilitate commerce and education, and allow access to independent media. Globalization can also create a framework for cooperation among nations on a range of non-economic issues that have cross-border implications, such as immigration, the environment, and legal issues. At the same time, the influx of foreign goods, services, and capital into a country can create incentives and demands for strengthening the education system, as a country's citizens recognize the competitive challenge before them.

Indeed, globalization's champions typically agree that the drive to increase productivity invites policy changes that benefit citizens in order to maintain economic progress. The result is that governments that embrace free markets find it difficult to restrict other liberties without jeopardizing the newly experienced economic growth. Richard Fisher, the president of the Federal Reserve Bank in Dallas, reports that his institution found that the governments themselves generally transform due to free trade reform. "In countries with a higher degree of globalization," Fisher asserts, "policies tend to support more accountability in the private and public sectors. These nations are more likely to maintain courts that recognize property rights and enforce the rule of law. Their governments are more effective and less corrupt."

The transmission of goods and services across national boundaries has accompanied a transmission of ideas and culture across these same borders. The expansion of the Internet, the reduction of international phone rates, and the growth of other communications technologies has brought cultures in greater contact with one another. Coupled with the relatively cheap price of international travel, these technologies have encouraged unprecedented levels of cultural exchange. People no longer remain merely citizens of their nation of origin but are fast becoming citizens of the world who are able to sample music, art, film, traditions, and other cultural expressions from many different lands. Some observers consider this broadening of personal identity as one of the profits of globalization. The United Nations Human Development Report of 2004 argues that rigidly adhering to the cultural expectations one is born into is becoming less desirable in a world that now offers opportunities to allow multicultural forces to shape one's identity. "People should not be bound in an immutable box called 'a culture'," the report asserts. "Cultural identities are heterogeneous and evolving—they are dynamic processes in which internal inconsistencies and conflicts drive change."

While some see this cultural exchange as a way to broaden perspectives, others contend that globalization is chiefly permitting a homogenization of culture—and one that is dominated by Western, primarily American, marketing. That is, many hitherto secluded cultures in Africa, Asia, Latin America, and the Middle East are being opened up to American goods and businesses. American food chains such as McDonald's can be found in nearly all parts of the globe, and American retail franchises are popping up in regions where thirty years ago they would have been unknown. Advertisements for Nike shoes or Coca-Cola are commonplace in foreign locales, and along with their enticement to buy a product is the invitation to buy into an Americanized lifestyle that values consumption.

Many critics of globalization see this push to expand American markets and values as a form of cultural imperialism—one that seeks to suppress foreign cultures in order to make more of the globe open to American products and the ideas that would encourage their continued dominance. The loss of indigenous traditions and values to this onslaught is disheartening to Jonathan Weber, a visiting professor of journalism at the University of Montana, who laments, "Even champions of globalization increasingly fret that [globalization] may damage or destroy the diversity that makes the human race so fascinating, leaving nothing but homogenized, least-common-denominator forms of creativity."

Along with the belief that it fosters a monoculture, critics of globalization question the supposed economic benefits of open markets. Most opponents argue that instead of promoting financial growth and consumer choice in developing nations, globalization is a means for economic powerhouses like the United States to dump excess production and make money on items that would otherwise go to waste. And with the rules that accompany free trade agreements, developing nations do not have the option to refuse these imports even if the flood would devastate local production. This practice commonly increases poverty and leaves many developing nations dependent on imports as local businesses fail.

Antiglobalization groups also claim that globalization has a detrimental effect on America and other economic giants. Most argue that the outsourcing of jobs to take advantage of cheap foreign labor simply robs developed economies of employment growth. The more information technology (IT) jobs shipped to India, the fewer positions left in the United States, for example. While outsourcing advocates would insist that money saved by exporting these "lost" positions allows companies to hire Americans to do other, often better, jobs, few critics believe that these better jobs ever materialize. In a 2006 article, economist Paul Craig Roberts maintains that regardless of the promises, "jobs outsourcing is not creating jobs in computer engineering and information technology" in the United States. Roberts claims that, instead, "the top ten sources of the most jobs in 'superpower' America are: retail salespersons, registered nurses, postsecondary teachers, customer service representatives, janitors and cleaners, waiters and waitresses, food preparation (includes fast food), home health aides, nursing aides, orderlies and attendants, general and operations managers." All of these are chiefly low-skill, low-paying service professions that do not produce goods that could be exported to relieve America's growing trade deficit. Roberts and others believe that as manufacturing and high-skill jobs leave U.S. shores, the living standard of all Americans will decline and the concept of upward mobility that underpins the American dream will disappear, polarizing the nation between the very rich and the predominantly poor.

Paul Craig Roberts is one of the many experts, analysts, and commentators whose viewpoints are shared within the pages of *Opposing Viewpoints: Globalization*. This anthology examines what these observers see as the pros and cons of both economic and cultural globalization. Their debate is carried out across four chapters that ask: How Does Globalization Affect World Society? What Is Globalization's Impact on World Crises? How Does Globalization Affect Developing Nations? and How Is Globalization Impacting the U.S. Economy? Both advocates and critics of globalization recognize that this force has already changed the way nations do business and even the way people across the globe interact, and each understands that the tide of globalization cannot be turned back. Their debate focuses on whether the pace of globalization is speeding its benefits or steamrolling over its pitfalls. And while this discussion will likely continue as globalization gains momentum, its main points of contention will surely depend on how everyone—individuals in developed and developing nations alike—weighs the costs of this modern phenomenon against the promises it fulfills.

OPPOSING
VIEWPOINTS®
SERIES

CHAPTER 1

How Does Globalization Affect World Society?

Chapter Preface

Many critics of globalization accuse economic free trade of forcing Western—or, more specifically, American—culture on the diverse populations of the world. In their view, freeing up global markets is simply a means for American products—from sneakers to foodstuffs to movies—to saturate foreign countries and dominate indigenous trade, traditions, and values. Advocates of globalization believe that the people of the world are just expressing their right to purchase the goods and entertainments they desire, but opponents contend that local crafts and cultural outlets simply cannot compete with the inundation of Western products. As university instructor Danny Duncan Collum writes in a 2007 issue of *Sojourners* magazine, globalization is "creating a global monoculture, dictated by the overwhelming economic power of the United States."

Some who decry the pervasive power of this Americanized monoculture not only fear what impact it may have on localized cultures but also what type of backlash it may provoke. As Jonathan Weber, a professor of journalism, wrote in *Wired* just five months after the September 11, 2001, al Qaeda terrorist attacks on the United States, anti-American sentiment may have much to do with exports—and the value system they promote—being foisted on unwilling consumers. "The fury of the terrorists—and of the alarming number of people around the world who viewed the attacks as a deserved comeuppance for an arrogant, out-of-control superpower," Weber stated, "is sparked in part by a sense that America is imposing its lifestyle on countries that don't want it. And one needn't condone mass murder to believe that a new world order that leaves every place on the globe looking like a California strip mall will make us all poorer."

Before the September 11 attacks, however, globalization's champions touted the way in which free trade brought people together, eroding the divisiveness that led to conflict. David Rothkopf, a professor of international affairs at Columbia University, speculated in *Foreign Policy* in 1997, "the decline of cultural distinctions may be a measure of the progress of civilization, a tangible sign of enhanced communications and understanding." And though in the post-9/11 world, few hype its power to level cultural distinctions, many promoters still claim globalization is enhancing communication and aiding cultural understanding through the global reach of the Internet and the international economic ties established through open markets. And most boosters see this cultural exchange as a two-way street, giving the economic powerhouses of the West a chance to learn from and sample the cultural offerings of once-distant and perhaps economically secluded nations in the developing world.

In the following chapter, the authors examine the impact of globalization on diverse cultures. Some see globalization as a bridge that connects populations, quelling old antagonisms and fostering new dialogues. Others, however, consider globalization as a steamroller, flattening indigenous cultures and inflaming a backlash against the threat of the oncoming monoculture.

> *"Governments that grant their citizens a large measure of freedom to engage in international commerce find it dauntingly difficult to deprive them of political and civil liberties."*

Globalization Promotes Democracy

Daniel T. Griswold

Daniel T. Griswold is director of the Center for Trade Policy Studies at the Cato Institute, a public policy organization that promotes free-market solutions. In the following viewpoint taken from a speech he gave at a trade conference in Norway, he argues that the world has become a safer place because of free trade and other globalization policies. In Griswold's view, opening nations economically allows more citizens to acquire goods and services and gives them a taste of what freedom of choice can provide. When more people share in the prosperity offered by free trade, they have more money to travel and communicate with the rest of the world, and they learn more about the liberties enjoyed in free nations, he contends, and adds that this makes them hungry for expanding freedoms at home and em-

Daniel T. Griswold, "Peace Through Trade" Conference, Center for Trade Policy Studies, April 20, 2007, Copyright © 2007 by Cato Institute. Republished with permission of Center for Trade Policy Studies, conveyed through Copyright Clearance Center, Inc.

bracing democratic rule. Griswold also maintains that global economic ties induce countries to abandon warfare in favor of peaceful, beneficial trade.

As you read, consider the following questions:

1. In Griswold's view, how does a growing middle class promote democracy in not-free nations?

2. Why does Griswold believe that imposing economic sanctions on not-free countries is a wrongheaded policy?

3. What are the three main ways in which free trade has promoted peace in the world, according to Griswold?

In Washington, as in Europe, trade policy is fought almost exclusively on the battlefield of bread and butter. What does it mean for exports, jobs, wages, and competition? At the Center for Trade Policy Studies, we think that the evidence is clear that trade benefits the U.S. economy and American families. Expanding trade, foreign investment and competition deliver lower prices, more choice and higher incomes for consumers. Globalization has opened fantastic opportunities for American and European companies to deliver goods and services to hundreds of millions of new customers in emerging markets.

The rising flow of capital across borders has raised returns for people who save and invest while funding new investment opportunities that spread good paying jobs and technologies around the globe. . . . But trade policy is also about the kind of wider world we want to live in.

A More Peaceful World

During the decades of the Cold War, Republican and Democratic presidents alike in the United States advocated international trade as a necessary tool for promoting human rights and democracy abroad, and ultimately a more peaceful world. Trade expansion was seen as an instrument not only for raising living standards but also for knitting together our Cold War allies and spreading the values and blessings of freedom to a wider circle of mankind. Trade was seen, rightly, as an instrument of peace in a world that had suffered two calamitous world wars only to face another totalitarian power in the Soviet Union.

This year [2007] marks the 60th anniversary of the founding of the General Agreement on Tariffs and Trade [GATT]. Sixty years ago [in 1947], representatives from 23 countries, including Norway and the United States, met in Geneva [Switzerland] to negotiate lower tariffs on goods within a framework of nondiscrimination and the rule of law. The participating countries understood all too clearly that the "beggar thy neighbor" protectionism of the 1930s had been an economic disaster. They also understood that economic warfare had deepened the despair and resentments that led to World War II.

In my remarks today, I want to go beyond bread and butter to talk about how free trade is tilling the soil for democracy and human rights around the world and how the expansion of economic liberty and democracy have done more than any army of U.N. blue helmets to promote peace.

Tilling Soil for Democracy

In one of my studies for Cato, called "Trading Tyranny for Freedom," I examined the idea of whether free and open markets promote human rights and democracy. Political scientists since Aristotle have long noted the connection between economic development, political reform, and democracy. Increased trade and economic integration promote civil and political freedoms directly by opening a society to new technology, communications, and democratic ideas. Along with the flow of consumer and industrial goods often come books, magazines, and other media with political and social content. Foreign investment and services trade create opportunities for foreign travel and study, allowing citizens to experience first-hand the civil liberties and more representative political institutions of other nations. Economic liberalization provides a counterweight to governmental power and creates space for civil society.

The faster growth and greater wealth that accompany trade promote democracy by creating an economically independent and politically aware middle class. A sizeable middle class means that more citizens can afford to be educated and take an interest in public affairs. They can afford cell phones, Internet access, and satellite TV. As citizens acquire assets and establish businesses and careers in the private sector, they prefer the continuity and evolutionary reform of a democratic system to the sharp turns and occasional revolutions of more authoritarian systems. People who are allowed to successfully manage their daily economic lives in a relatively free market come to expect and demand more freedom in the political and social realm.

Wealth by itself does not promote democracy if the wealth is controlled by the state or a small, ruling elite. That's why a number of oil-rich countries in the Middle East and elsewhere remain politically repressive despite their relatively high per capita incomes. For wealth to cultivate the soil for democracy, it must be produced, retained, and controlled by a broad base of society, and for wealth to be created in that manner, an economy must be relatively open and free.

Freedom Is Spreading

In my study for Cato, I found that the reality of the world broadly reflects those theoretical links between trade, free markets, and political and civil freedom.

First, I examined the broad global trends in both trade and political liberty during the past three decades. Since the early 1970s, cross-border flows of trade, investment, and currency have increased dramatically, and far faster than output

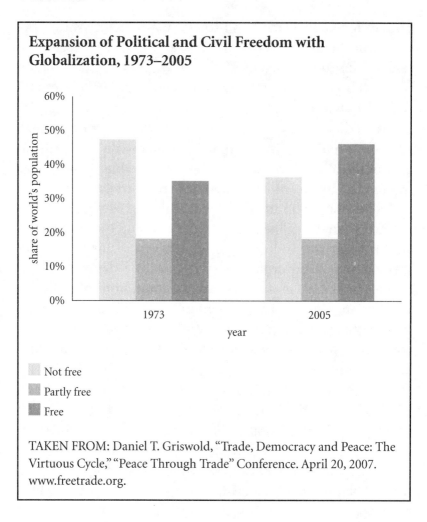

Expansion of Political and Civil Freedom with Globalization, 1973–2005

share of world's population

- Not free
- Partly free
- Free

TAKEN FROM: Daniel T. Griswold, "Trade, Democracy and Peace: The Virtuous Cycle," "Peace Through Trade" Conference. April 20, 2007. www.freetrade.org.

itself. Trade barriers have fallen unilaterally and through multilateral and regional trade agreements in Latin America, in the former Soviet bloc nations, in East Asia, including China, and in more developed nations as well. During that same period, political and civil liberties have been spreading around the world. Thirty years ago democracies were the exception in Latin America, while today they are the rule. Many former communist states from the old Soviet Union and its empire have successfully transformed themselves into functioning democracies that protect basic civil and political freedoms. In

East Asia, democracy and respect for human rights have re-placed authoritarian rule in South Korea, Taiwan, the Philippines, and Indonesia.

Freedom House, a human rights think tank in New York, measures the political and civil freedom each year in every country in the world. It classifies countries into three categories: "Free"—meaning countries where citizens enjoy the freedom to vote as well as full freedom of the press, speech, religion and independent civic life; "Partly Free"—those countries "in which there is limited respect for political rights and civil liberties"; and "Not Free"—"where basic political rights are absent and basic civil liberties are widely and systematically denied." According to the most recent Freedom House survey, political and civil freedoms have expanded dramatically along with the spread of globalization and freer trade. In 1973, 35 percent of the world's population lived in countries that were "Free." Today that share has increased to 46 percent. In 1973, almost half of the people in the world, 47 percent, lived in countries that were "Not Free." Today that share has mercifully fallen to 36 percent. The share of people living in countries that are "Partly Free" is the same, 18 percent.

In other words, in the past three decades, more than one-tenth of humanity has escaped the darkest tyranny for the bright sunlight of civil and political freedom. That represents 700 million people who once suffered under the jack boot of oppression who now enjoy the same civil and political liberties that we all take for granted.

Strengthening Human Rights

Next, I examined the relationship between economic openness in individual countries today and their record of human rights and democracy. To make this comparison, I combined the Freedom House ratings with the ratings for economic freedom contained in the Economic Freedom of the World Report. That study rates more than 120 countries according to the freedom to trade and invest internationally, to engage in business, access to sound money, property rights, and the size of government. The study is jointly sponsored by 50 think tanks around the world, including the Cato Institute, the Fraser Institute in Canada, and Norway's own Center for Business and Society Incorporated, or Civita. When we compare political and civil freedoms to economic freedom, we find that nations with open and free economies are far more likely to enjoy full political and civil liberties than those with closed and state-dominated economies. Of the 25 rated countries in the top quintile of economic openness, 21 are rated "Free" by Freedom House and only one is rated "Not Free." In contrast, among the quintile of countries that are the least open economically, only seven are rated "Free" and nine are rated "Not Free." In other words, the most economically open countries are three times more likely to enjoy full political and civil freedoms as those that are economically closed. Those that are closed are nine times more likely to completely suppress civil and political freedoms as those that are open.

The percentage of countries rated as "Free" rises in each quintile as the freedom to exchange with foreigners rises, while the percentage rated as "Not Free" falls. In fact, 17 of the 20 countries rated as "Not Free" are found in the bottom two quintiles of economic openness, and only three in the top three quintiles. The percentage of nations rated as "Partly Free" also drops precipitously in the top two quintiles of economic openness.

A more formal statistical comparison shows a significant, positive correlation between economic freedom, including the freedom to engage in international commerce, and political and civil freedom. The statistical correlation remains strong even when controlling for a nation's per capita gross domestic product [GDP], consistent with the theory that economic openness reinforces political liberty directly and independently of its effect on growth and income levels. One unmistakable lesson from the cross-country data is that governments that grant their citizens a large measure of freedom to engage in international commerce find it dauntingly difficult to deprive them of political and civil liberties. A corollary lesson is that governments that "protect" their citizens behind tariff walls and other barriers to international commerce find it much easier to deny those same liberties.

Even when we look at reform within individual countries, we see a connection. A statistical analysis of those countries shows a significant and positive correlation between the expansion of the freedom to exchange with foreigners over the past three decades in individual countries and an expansion of political and civil freedoms in the same country during the same period. Countries that have most aggressively followed those twin tracks of reform—reflected in their improved scores during the past two decades in the indexes for freedom of exchange and combined political and civil freedom—include Chile, Ghana, Hungary, Mexico, Nicaragua, Paraguay, Portugal, and Tanzania. Twenty years ago, both South Korea and Taiwan were essentially one-party states without free elections or full civil liberties. Today, due in large measure to economic liberalization, trade reform, and the economic growth they spurred, both are thriving democracies where a large and well-educated middle class enjoys the full range of civil liberties. In both countries, opposition parties have gained political power against long-time ruling parties.

Our best hope for political reform in countries that are "Not Free" will not come from confrontation and economic sanctions. In Cuba, for example, expanded trade with the United States would be a far more promising policy to bring an end to the Castro era than the failed, four-decades-old economic embargo. Based on experience elsewhere, the U.S. government could more effectively promote political and civil freedom in Cuba by allowing more trade and travel than by maintaining the embargo. The folly of imposing trade sanctions in the name of promoting human rights abroad is that sanctions deprive people in the target countries of the technological tools and economic opportunities that nurture political freedom.

A More Democratic China

In China, the link between trade and political reform offers the best hope for encouraging democracy and greater respect for human rights in the world's most populous nation. After two decades of reform and rapid growth, an expanding middle class is experiencing for the first time the independence of home ownership, travel abroad, and cooperation with others in economic enterprise free of government control. The number of telephone lines, mobile phones, and Internet users has risen exponentially in the past decade. Tens of thousands of Chinese students are studying abroad each year.

China's entry into the World Trade Organization in 2001 has only accelerated those trends.

So far, the people of mainland China have seen only marginal improvements in civil liberties and none in political liberties. But the people of China are undeniably less oppressed than they were during the tumult of the Cultural Revolution under Mao Tse-tung. And China is reaching the stage of development where countries tend to shed oppressive forms of government for more benign and democratic systems. China's per capita GDP has reached about $7,600 per in terms of purchasing power parity. That puts China in the upper half of the world's countries and in an income neighborhood where more people live in political and civil freedom and fewer under tyranny. Among countries with lower per capita incomes than China, only 27 percent are free. Among those with higher incomes, 72 percent are free. Only 16 percent are not free, and almost all of those are wealthier than China not because of greater economic freedom but because of oil.

By multiple means of measurement, political and civil freedoms do correlate in the real world with expanding freedom to trade and transact across international borders. Nations that have opened their economies over time are indeed more likely to have opened themselves to political competition and greater freedom for citizens to speak, assemble, and worship freely. And around the globe, the broad expansion of international trade and investment has accompanied an equally broad expansion of democracy and the political and civil freedoms it is supposed to protect.

The Peace Dividend

The good news does not stop there. Buried beneath the daily stories about suicide bombings and insurgency movements is an underappreciated but encouraging fact: The world has somehow become a more peaceful place.

A little-noticed headline on an Associated Press story a while back reported, "War declining worldwide, studies say." In 2006, a survey by the Stockholm International Peace Research Institute found that the number of armed conflicts around the world has been in decline for the past half-century. Since the early 1990s, ongoing conflicts have dropped from 33 to 17, with all of them now civil conflicts within countries. The Institute's latest report found that 2005 marked the second year in a row that no two nations were at war with one another. What a remarkable and wonderful fact.

The death toll from war has also been falling. According to the Associated Press report, "The number killed in battle has fallen to its lowest point in the post–World War II period, dipping below 20,000 a year by one measure. Peacemaking missions, meanwhile, are growing in number." Current estimates of people killed by war are down sharply from annual tolls ranging from 40,000 to 100,000 in the 1990s, and from a peak of 700,000 in 1951 during the Korean War.

Many causes lie behind the good news—the end of the Cold War and the spread of democracy, among them—but expanding trade and globalization appear to be playing a major role in promoting world peace. Far from stoking a "World on Fire," as one misguided American author argued in a forgettable book, growing commercial ties between nations have had a dampening effect on armed conflict and war. I would argue that free trade and globalization have promoted peace in three main ways.

First, as I argued a moment ago, trade and globalization have reinforced the trend toward democracy, and democracies tend not to pick fights with each other. Thanks in part to globalization, almost two thirds of the world's countries today are democracies—a record high. Some studies have cast doubt on the idea that democracies are less likely to fight wars. While it's true that democracies rarely if ever war with each other, it is not such a rare occurrence for democracies to engage in wars with non-democracies. We can still hope that as more countries turn to democracy, there will be fewer provocations for war by non-democracies.

A second and even more potent way that trade has promoted peace is by promoting more economic integration. As national economies become more intertwined with each other, those nations have more to lose should war break out. War in a globalized world not only means human casualties and bigger government, but also ruptured trade and investment ties that impose lasting damage on the economy. In short, globalization has dramatically raised the economic cost of war. . . .

A third reason why free trade promotes peace is because it allows nations to acquire wealth through production and exchange rather than conquest of territory and resources. As economies develop, wealth is increasingly measured in terms of intellectual property, financial assets, and human capital. Such assets cannot be easily seized by armies. In contrast, hard assets such as minerals and farmland are becoming relatively less important in a high-tech, service economy. If people need resources outside their national borders, say oil or timber or farm products, they can acquire them peacefully by trading away what they can produce best at home. In short, globalization and the development it has spurred have rendered the spoils of war less valuable.

Of course, free trade and globalization do not guarantee peace. Hot-blooded nationalism and ideological fervor can overwhelm cold economic calculations. Any relationship involving human beings will be messy and non-linear. There will always be exceptions and outliers in such complex relationships involving economies and governments. But deep trade and investment ties among nations make war less attractive.

A Grand, Virtuous Cycle

The global trends we've witnessed in the spread of trade, democracy and peace tend to reinforce each other in a grand and virtuous cycle. As trade and development encourage more representative government, those governments provide more predictability and incremental reform, creating a better climate for trade and investment to flourish. And as the spread of trade and democracy foster peace, the decline of war creates a more hospitable environment for trade and economic growth and political stability.

We can see this virtuous cycle at work in the world today. The European Union just celebrated its 50th birthday. For many of the same non-economic reasons that motivated the founders of the GATT, the original members of the European community hoped to build a more sturdy foundation for peace. Out of the ashes of World War II, the United States urged Germany, France and other Western European nations to form a common market that has become the European Union. In large part because of their intertwined economies, a general war in Europe is now unthinkable.

In East Asia, the extensive and growing economic ties among Mainland China, Japan, South Korea, and Taiwan is helping to keep the peace. China's communist rulers may yet decide to go to war over its "renegade province [Taiwan]," but the economic cost to their economy would be staggering and could provoke a backlash among its citizens. In contrast, poor and isolated North Korea is all the more dangerous because it has nothing to lose economically should it provoke a war.

In Central America, countries that were racked by guerrilla wars and death squads two decades ago have turned not only to democracy but to expanding trade, culminating in the Central American Free Trade Agreement with the United States. As the Stockholm Institute reported in its 2005 Yearbook, "Since the 1980s, the introduction of a more open economic model in most states of the Latin American and Caribbean region has been accompanied by the growth of new regional structures, the dying out of interstate conflicts and a reduction in intra-state conflicts."

Much of the political violence that remains in the world today is concentrated in the Middle East and Sub-Saharan Africa—the two regions of the world that are the least integrated into the global economy. Efforts to bring peace to those regions must include lowering their high barriers to trade, foreign investment, and entrepreneurship.

Finally, those of us who live in countries that have benefited the most from free trade and globalization should rededicate ourselves to expanding and institutionalizing the freedom to trade.

| "*Globalization is a logical extension of imperialism.*"

Globalization Undermines Democracy

Michael Parenti

In the following viewpoint, Michael Parenti argues that free trade subverts democracy because it privileges the rights of corporations over the national rights of citizens. Parenti claims that free trade agreements are made without popular or legislative consent, yet the provisions of such agreements often take precedence over the economic rights and other personal liberties guaranteed by national constitutions. For this reason, Parenti believes globalization erodes national sovereignty and runs contrary to the democratic process. Michael Parenti is a political analyst and lecturer who has written several books, including Democracy for the Few *and* The Cultural Struggle.

As you read, consider the following questions:

1. Why does Parenti believe that free trade does not equate with fair trade?

Michael Parenti, "Globalization and Democracy: Some Basics," CommonDreams.org, May 26, 2007. Reproduced by permission of the author.

2. According to Parenti, what happened under NAFTA when Mexico was flooded with cheap, high-tech corn stocks from the United States?

3. In Parenti's view, how are free trade agreements in violation of the U.S. Constitution?

The goal of the transnational corporation is to become truly transnational, poised above the sovereign power of any particular nation, while being served by the sovereign powers of all nations. Cyril Siewert, chief financial officer of Colgate Palmolive Company, could have been speaking for all transnationals when he remarked, "The United States doesn't have an automatic call on our [corporation's] resources. There is no mindset that puts this country first."

With international "free trade" agreements such as NAFTA [North American Free Trade Agreement], GATT [General Agreement on Tariffs and Trade], and FTAA [Free Trade Area of the Americas], the giant transnationals have been elevated above the sovereign powers of nation states. These agreements endow anonymous international trade committees with the authority to prevent, overrule, or dilute any laws of any nation deemed to burden the investment and market prerogatives of transnational corporations. These trade committees—of which the World Trade Organization (WTO) is a prime example—set up panels composed of "trade specialists" who act as judges over economic issues, placing themselves above the rule and popular control of any nation, thereby insuring the supremacy of international finance capital. This process, called *globalization*, is treated as an inevitable natural "growth" development beneficial to all. It is in fact a global coup d'état by the giant business interests of the world.

Nations Must Bow to Corporations

Elected by no one and drawn from the corporate world, these panelists meet in secret and often have investment stakes in the very issues they adjudicate, being bound by no conflict-of-interest provisions. Not one of GATT's five hundred pages of rules and restrictions are directed against private corporations; all are against governments. Signatory governments must lower tariffs, end farm subsidies, treat foreign companies the same as domestic ones, honor all corporate patent claims, and obey the rulings of a permanent elite bureaucracy, the WTO [World Trade Organization]. Should a country refuse to change its laws when a WTO panel so dictates, the WTO can impose fines or international trade sanctions, depriving the resistant country of needed markets and materials.

Acting as the supreme global adjudicator, the WTO has ruled against laws deemed "barriers to free trade." It has forced Japan to accept greater pesticide residues in imported food. It has kept Guatemala from outlawing deceptive advertising of baby food. It has eliminated the ban in various countries on asbestos, and on fuel-economy and emission standards for motor vehicles. And it has ruled against marine-life protection laws and the ban on endangered-species products. The European Union's prohibition on the importation of hormone-ridden U.S. beef had overwhelming popular support throughout Europe, but a three-member WTO panel decided the ban was an illegal restraint on trade. The decision on beef put in jeopardy a host of other food import regulations based on health concerns. The WTO overturned a portion of the U.S. Clean Air Act banning certain additives in gasoline because it interfered with imports from foreign refineries. And the WTO overturned that portion of the U.S. Endangered Species Act forbidding the import of shrimp caught with nets that failed to protect sea turtles.

Globalization Trumps Rights and Freedoms

Free trade is not fair trade; it benefits strong nations at the expense of weaker ones, and rich interests at the expense of the rest of us. Globalization means turning the clock back on many twentieth-century reforms: no freedom to boycott products, no prohibitions against child labor, no guaranteed living wage or benefits, no public services that might conceivably compete with private services, no health and safety protections that might cut into corporate profits.

GATT and subsequent free trade agreements allow multinationals to impose monopoly property rights on indigenous and communal agriculture. In this way agribusiness can better penetrate locally self-sufficient communities and monopolize their resources. [Consumer advocate] Ralph Nader gives the example of the neem tree, whose extracts contain natural pesticidal and medicinal properties. Cultivated for centuries in India, the tree attracted the attention of various pharmaceutical companies, who filed monopoly patents, causing mass protests by Indian farmers. As dictated by the WTO, the pharmaceuticals now have exclusive control over the marketing of neem tree products, a ruling that is being reluctantly enforced in India. Tens of thousands of erstwhile independent farmers must now work for the powerful pharmaceuticals on profit-gorging terms set by the companies.

A trade agreement between India and the United States, the Knowledge Initiative on Agriculture (KIA), backed by Monsanto and other transnational corporate giants, allows for the grab of India's seed sector by Monsanto, its trade sector by Archer Daniels Midland and Cargill, and its retail sector by Wal-Mart. (Wal-Mart announced plans to open 500 stores in India, starting in August 2007.) This amounts to a war against India's independent farmers and small businesses, and a threat to India's food security. Farmers are organizing to protect themselves against this economic invasion by maintaining traditional seed-banks and setting up systems of communal agrarian support. One farmer says, "We do not buy seeds from the market because we suspect they may be contaminated with genetically engineered or terminator seeds."

In a similar vein, the WTO ruled that the U.S. corporation RiceTec has the patent rights to all the many varieties of basmati rice, grown for centuries by India's farmers. It also ruled that a Japanese corporation had exclusive rights in the world to grow and produce curry powder. As these instances demonstrate, what is called "free trade" amounts to international corporate monopoly control. Such developments caused Malaysian prime minister Mahathir Mohamad to observe:

> We now have a situation where theft of genetic resources by western biotech TNCs [transnational corporations] enables them to make huge profits by producing patented genetic mutations of these same materials. What depths have we sunk to in the global marketplace when nature's gifts to the poor may not be protected but their modifications by the rich become exclusive property?

Markets Set the Rules

If the current behavior of the rich countries is anything to go by, globalization simply means the breaking down of the borders of countries so that those with the capital and the goods will be free to dominate the markets.

Under free-trade agreements like General Agreements on Trade and Services (GATS) and Free Trade Area of the Americas (FTAA), all public services are put at risk. A public service can be charged with causing "lost market opportunities" for business, or creating an unfair subsidy. To offer one instance: the single-payer automobile insurance program proposed by the province of Ontario, Canada, was declared "unfair competition." Ontario could have its public auto insurance only if it paid U.S. insurance companies what they estimated would be their present and *future* losses in Ontario auto insurance sales, a prohibitive cost for the province. Thus the citizens of Ontario were not allowed to exercise their democratic sovereign right to institute an alternative not-for-profit auto insurance system. In another case, United P[arce]l Service charged the

Canadian Post Office for "lost market opportunities," which means that under free trade accords, the Canadian Post Office would have to compensate UPS for all the business that UPS thinks it would have had if there were no public postal service. The Canadian postal workers union has challenged the case in court, arguing that the agreement violates the Canadian Constitution.

Under NAFTA, the U.S.-based Ethyl Corporation sued the Canadian government for $250 million in "lost business opportunities" and "interference with trade" because Canada banned MMT, an Ethyl-produced gasoline additive considered carcinogenic by Canadian officials. Fearing they would lose the case, Canadian officials caved in, agreeing to lift the ban on MMT, pay Ethyl $10 million compensation, and issue a public statement calling MMT "safe," even though they had scientific findings showing otherwise. California also banned the unhealthy additive; this time a Canadian-based Ethyl company sued California under NAFTA for placing an unfair burden on free trade.

International free trade agreements like GATT and NAFTA have hastened the corporate acquisition of local markets, squeezing out smaller businesses and worker collectives. Under NAFTA better-paying U.S. jobs were lost as firms closed shop and contracted out to the cheaper Mexican labor market. At the same time thousands of Mexican small companies were forced out of business. Mexico was flooded with cheap, high-tech, mass produced corn and dairy products from giant U.S. agribusiness firms (themselves heavily subsidized by the U.S. government), driving small Mexican farmers and distributors into bankruptcy, displacing large numbers of poor peasants. The lately arrived U.S. companies in Mexico have offered extremely low-paying jobs, and unsafe work conditions. Generally free trade has brought a dramatic increase in poverty south of the border.

Governments Seem Powerless to Act

We North Americans are told that to remain competitive in the new era of globalization, we will have to increase our output while reducing our labor and production costs, in other words, work harder for less. This in fact is happening as the work-week has lengthened by as much as twenty percent (from forty hours to forty-six and even forty-eight hours) and real wages have flattened or declined during the reign of George W. Bush. Less is being spent on social services, and we are enduring more wage concessions, more restructuring, deregulation, and privatization. Only with such "adjustments," one hears, can we hope to cope with the impersonal forces of globalization that are sweeping us along.

In fact, there is nothing impersonal about these forces. Free trade agreements, including new ones that have not yet been submitted to the U.S. Congress have been consciously planned by big business and its government minions over a period of years in pursuit of a deregulated world economy that undermines all democratic checks upon business practices. The people of any one province, state, or nation are now finding it increasingly difficult to get their governments to impose protective regulations or develop new forms of public sector production out of fear of being overruled by some self-appointed international free-trade panel.

Usually it is large nations demanding that poorer smaller ones relinquish the protections and subsidies they provide for their local producers. But occasionally things may take a different turn. Thus in late 2006 Canada launched a dispute at the World Trade Organization over the use of "trade-distorting" agricultural subsidies by the United States, specifically the enormous sums dished out by the federal government to U.S. agribusiness corn farmers. The case also challenged the entire multibillion-dollar structure of U.S. agricultural subsidies. It followed the landmark WTO ruling of 2005 which condemned "trade-distorting" aid to U.S. cotton farmers. A report by Oxfam International revealed that at least thirty-eight developing countries were suffering severely as a result of trade distorting subsidies by both the United States and the European Union. Meanwhile, the U.S. government was maneuvering to insert a special clause into trade negotiations that would place its illegal use of farm subsidies above challenge by WTO member countries and make the subsidies immune from adjudication through the WTO dispute settlement process.

Excluding Congress, Excluding the People

What is seldom remarked upon is that NAFTA and GATT are in violation of the U.S. Constitution, the preamble of which makes clear that sovereign power rests with the people: "We the People of the United States . . . do ordain and establish this Constitution for the United States of America." Article I, Section 1 of the Constitution reads, "All legislative Powers herein granted shall be vested in a Congress of the United States." Article I, Section 7 gives the president (not some trade council) the power to veto a law, subject to being overridden by a two-thirds vote in Congress. And Article III gives adjudication and review powers to a Supreme Court and other federal courts as ordained by Congress. The Tenth Amendment to the Constitution states: "The powers not delegated to the United States by the Constitution, nor prohibited by it to the States, are reserved to the States respectively, or to the people." There is nothing in the entire Constitution that allows an international trade panel to preside as final arbiter exercising supreme review powers undermining the constitutionally mandated decisions of the legislative, executive, and judicial branches.

True, Article VII says that the Constitution, federal laws, and treaties "shall be the supreme Law of the land," but certainly this was not intended to include treaties that overrode

Mistaking Capitalism for Democracy

Why has capitalism succeeded while democracy has steadily weakened? Democracy has become enfeebled largely because companies, in intensifying competition for global consumers and investors, have invested ever greater sums in lobbying, public relations, and even bribes and kickbacks, seeking laws that give them a competitive advantage over their rivals. The result is an arms race for political influence that is drowning out the voices of average citizens. In the United States, for example, the fights that preoccupy Congress, those that consume weeks or months of congressional staff time, are typically contests between competing companies or industries.

While corporations are increasingly writing their own rules, they are also being entrusted with a kind of social responsibility or morality. Politicians praise companies for acting "responsibly" or condemn them for not doing so. Yet the purpose of capitalism is to get great deals for consumers and investors. Corporate executives are not authorized by anyone—least of all by their investors—to balance profits against the public good. Nor do they have any expertise in making such moral calculations.

Robert B. Reich, Foreign Policy, *September/October 2007.*

the laws themselves and the sovereign democratic power of the people and their representatives.

To exclude the Senate from deliberations, NAFTA and GATT were called "agreements" instead of treaties, a semantic ploy that enabled President [Bill] Clinton to bypass the two-thirds treaty ratification vote in the Senate and avoid any treaty amendment process. The World Trade Organization was approved by a lame-duck session of Congress held after the

1994 elections. No one running in that election uttered a word to voters about putting the U.S. government under a perpetual obligation to ensure that national laws do not conflict with international free trade rulings.

What is being undermined is not only a lot of good laws dealing with environment, public services, labor standards, and consumer protection, but also *the very right to legislate such laws.* Our democratic sovereignty itself is being surrendered to a secretive plutocratic trade organization that presumes to exercise a power greater than that of the people and their courts and legislatures. What we have is an international coup d'état by big capital over the nations of the world.

Globalization Builds Corporate Empires

Globalization is a logical extension of imperialism, a victory of empire over republic, international finance capital over local productivity and nation-state democracy (such as it is). In recent times however, given popular protests, several multilateral trade agreements have been stalled or voted down. In 1999, militant protests against free trade took place in forty-one nations from Britain and France to Thailand and India. In 2000–01, there were demonstrations in Seattle, Washington, Sydney, Prague, Genoa, and various other locales. In 2003–04 we saw the poorer nations catching wise to the free trade scams and refusing to sign away what shreds of sovereignty they still had. Along with the popular resistance, more national leaders are thinking twice before signing on to new trade agreements.

The discussion of globalization by some Marxists (but not all) has focused on the question of whether the new "internationalization" of capital will undermine national sovereignty and the nation state. They dwell on this question while leaving unmentioned such things as free trade agreements and the WTO. Invariably these observers (for instance Ellen Wood and William Taab in *Monthly Review*, Ian Jasper in *Nature, Society and Thought,* Erwin Marquit in *Political Affairs*) conclude that the nation state still plays a key role in capitalist imperialism, that capital—while global in its scope—is not international but bound to particular nations, and that globalization is little more than another name for overseas monopoly capital investment.

They repeatedly remind us that Marx had described globalization, this process of international financial expansion, as early as 1848, when he and Engels in the *Communist Manifesto* wrote about how capitalism moves into all corners of the world, reshaping all things into its own image. Therefore, there is no cause for the present uproar. Globalization, these writers conclude, is not a new development but a longstanding one that Marxist theory uncovered long ago.

The problem with this position is that it misses the whole central point of the current struggle. It is not only *national* sovereignty that is at stake, it is *democratic* sovereignty. Millions of people all over the world have taken to the streets to protest free trade agreements. Among them are farmers, workers, students and intellectuals (including many Marxists who see things more clearly than the aforementioned ones), all of whom are keenly aware that something new is afoot and they want no part of it. As used today, the term *globalization* refers to a new stage of international expropriation, designed not to put an end to the nation-state but to undermine whatever democratic right exists to protect the social wage and restrain the power of transnational corporations.

Free Trade Is Anything but Free

The free trade agreements, in effect, make unlawful all statutes and regulations that restrict private capital in any way. Carried to full realization, this means the end of whatever imperfect democratic protections the populace has been able to muster after generations of struggle in the realm of public policy. Under the free trade agreements any and all public services can be ruled out of existence because they cause "lost market opportunities" for private capital. So too public hospitals can be charged with taking away markets from private hospitals; and public water supply systems, public schools, public libraries, public housing and public transportation are guilty of depriving their private counterparts of market opportunities, likewise public health insurance, public mail delivery, and public auto insurance systems. Laws that try to protect the environment or labor standards or consumer health already have been overthrown for "creating barriers" to free trade.

What also is overthrown is the *right* to have such laws. This is the most important point of all and the one most frequently overlooked by persons from across the political spectrum. Under the free trade accords, property rights have been elevated to international supremacy, able to take precedent over all other rights, including the right to a clean, livable environment, the right to affordable public services, and the right to any morsel of economic democracy. Instead a new right has been accorded absolutist status, the right to corporate private profit. It has been used to stifle the voice of working people and their ability to develop a public sector that serves their interests. Free speech itself is undermined as when "product disparagement" is treated as an interference with free trade. And nature itself is being monopolized and privatized by transnational corporations.

So the fight against free trade is a fight for the right to politico-economic democracy, public services, and a social wage, the right not to be completely at the mercy of big capital. It is a new and drastic phase of the class struggle that some Marxists—so immersed in classical theory and so ill-informed about present-day public policy—seem to have missed. As embodied in the free trade accords, globalization has little to do with trade and is anything but free. It benefits the rich nations over poor ones, and the rich classes within all nations at the expense of ordinary citizens. It is the new specter that haunts the same old world.

"It will be faith—be it traditional or otherwise—that will bring people together in the future."

Globalization Encourages People to Identify Themselves Along Religious Lines

Arun Pereira

Arun Pereira is a professor of business marketing at Saint Louis University in Missouri. In the viewpoint that follows, Pereira claims that globalization is breaking down national borders and inviting mass immigration based on finding better economic opportunities. This, in Pereira's view, will undermine nationalism and leave largely ethnically diversified societies without unity. Pereira expects that religion will step in to replace national identity as the rallying point for the various groups that are dispersed across the globalized world.

As you read, consider the following questions:

1. Why does Pereira believe that the West has yet to experience the "identity crisis" many migrants from the developing world are experiencing as a result of globalization?

Arun Pereira, "The Rally Round Religion: Globalization Is Making Faith, Not Nationality, People's Primary Identity," *National Catholic Reporter*, August 8, 2008. Reproduced by permission of National Catholic Reporter, www.natcath.org.

2. As Pereira relates, how does Stanley Kober use the breakup of Yugoslavia as an example of what may happen to disintegrating nation-states in the era of globalization?

3. Why does Pereira contend that immigrant groups today have little incentive to assimilate into the dominant cultures of adopted nations?

A time of expanding global trade, new technologies disseminating information in unprecedented ways, and religious fanaticism forcing people to take up arms—yes, the 16th century was a momentous period that saw a surge in globalization, the invention of the printing press, and wars driven by religious fanatics. It also saw the unraveling of a unique alliance between the popes and the emperors, the so-called Holy Roman Empire, after eight centuries of mutually beneficial—and sometimes uneasy—collaboration. That alliance and its unraveling may have important implications for the present time, particularly as the world experiences unprecedented levels of immigration and grapples with difficult challenges in the assimilation of immigrants.

A History Lesson

Beginning with Charlemagne in A.D. 800, the emperors of the Holy Roman Empire used religion—through the papacy—to wield power over subjects spread over various principalities and fiefdoms in Western and Central Europe. Charlemagne and his successors were officially crowned by the popes, thereby bestowing a spiritual legitimacy to their reigns. In return, the pope received security and protection. The emperors recognized the power of religion to unify diverse subjects—people of various ethnicities and social classes, speaking languages that varied from German and its dialects to the Slavic languages.

This strategy worked because Europe was going through a tumultuous period characterized by changing emperors and kings, shifting boundaries among fiefdoms, and people on the move. Under these ever-changing conditions, individual identity was shaped by the one constant in people's lives: religion. Allegiance to religion bested all other loyalties such as allegiance to emperors, barons, and even ethnicity, language and social class.

Today in most parts of the world people are undergoing unparalleled change, driven by the effects of globalization. We are witnessing the greatest wave of migration in the history of the world. According to the International Migration Organization, there were nearly 200 million immigrants worldwide in 2005, a number that equals the fifth-most populous country in the world. Even as we see efforts in the United States and Western Europe to deter illegal immigration, the forces of globalization are driving legal immigration to levels never seen before. Globalization is changing the structure of the world economy, with nation-states giving way to giant trade blocs and national borders being redefined or erased. All these factors fundamentally undermine patriotism and national identity.

Rootless Pilgrims

People in the West may not appreciate or recognize this "identity crisis" because they have yet to fully experience the wrenching consequences of globalization affecting those in the developing world. Consider today's global immigrants. Where do the identity and allegiance of a new immigrant lie? Nation of birth? Nation of present residence? A giant trade bloc? This is a crucial question because individual identity is fundamental to how conflicts start. According to Stanley Kober, a research fellow in foreign policy studies at the CATO Institute, "Wars begin in people's minds—and are rooted in how they view other people. Put simply, people do not kill people with whom they identify." In a borderless world wrought by continuous instability and change, with what or whom does one identify?

History would suggest that just like during the Holy Roman Empire, people's identities and loyalties are increasingly tied to the one constant in their lives: religion, be it one of the established faiths or otherwise. So much so, they are likely to put their lives on the line for religion more readily than for any other cause. As an example, Kober offers the breakup of Yugoslavia. Its citizens coalesced into countries based on religion: Muslim Bosnia, Orthodox Serbia, Catholic Croatia. More telling was the pattern of international sympathy for these new nations; Germany, the kingpin of the erstwhile Holy Roman Empire, led the way for the early recognition of Catholic Croatia, as did Greece and Russia for Orthodox Serbia, and a host of Islamic nations for Muslim Bosnia.

It is a matter of time before the full effects of this identity crisis hit the West. As national borders continue to fall and more trade blocs emerge, the people in the West will join the migrating masses, moving from one economic opportunity to another, tied to very little but their religious faiths. In the future, even if you don't move, much of the world's population will be doing so, fundamentally affecting you and forcing you to confront the basis of your national identity. We already see this in Europe where a growing Muslim population is causing Europeans to take a closer look at their Christian roots. In the United States, if non-European, non-Christian immigrants come in great numbers as they are already starting to do, many Americans will also feel a need to defend and emphasize the "Christian" identity of the United States. Americans will react like the rest of the world, rallying around their religious faith and fiercely protecting it. It may be the aspect of their identity that Americans prove unwilling to compromise on, even as they adapt to and tolerate the changing face of their country in terms of skin colors, languages and cultures. In the

Religious Community Is Stronger

While modernisation sought to eradicate traditional or religious patterns of behaviour in the name of rational change, nation building on the basis of secular citizenship does not appear to have been entirely successful, because the nation is an imaginary community that requires sacred symbols, myths and practices to reproduce its coherence and authority. Colonialism often destroyed the historical relationship between religion and community, but was unable to replace the organic relationship between community and sacred power. Secular citizenship became the preferred model of civil society politics in the era of nationalism, but globalisation has brought into question the relevance of (national) citizenship for modern politics, while religion, precisely because it is not a manifestation of the nation, may have more relevance to identity formation in the process of cultural globalisation.

Bryan S. Turner, Asian Journal of Social Science, *2006.*

extreme, a "brown" America (or even a "Spanish" America) will likely be tolerated but not a Muslim America, or a Hindu America.

Disillusioned Faithful

There is little incentive for today's immigrants to completely assimilate in the host country because their sheer numbers make it easier for them to hold on to their old ways, traditions and loyalties. By not assimilating comprehensively, the immigrants are perceived to be "different" and thus less welcome by existing citizens, further alienating the new immigrants and producing even less integration. The end result is that new immigrants don't completely accept their new country as home, and for the existing citizens it feels less like home because of the changing character of their country. However, even under these conditions, you can be sure that people—new immigrants, old immigrants, natives—would stand, kneel and sit shoulder to shoulder at the church, mosque or temple, listening as one to their religious leaders. Or in many cases, disillusioned by traditional, organized religion, they are drawn to other breakaway sects and variations of religion, sometimes called "New Age spirituality," served by a number of charismatic leaders. Regardless, it will be faith—be it traditional or otherwise—that will bring people together in the future, not the Stars and Stripes or the Union Jack.

Tomorrow's superpowers will not have physical boundaries; their boundaries will be those of the mind and soul. In fact, it will be countries or trade blocs that will divide the faithful of various religions with ever-changing physical borders. And it will be religions—traditional, organized or otherwise—that will unite the far-flung faithful. Those with strong and charismatic leaders will be able to affect and influence the behavior of vast numbers of people, and therefore our world. The mantle of power will fall on religious leaders, be they benevolent and selfless, or power-hungry renegades. It is the likes of Pope Benedict XVI and, yes, even maniacal individuals like [al Qaeda leader] Osama bin Laden who will have increasing power to influence our world.

Opportunity for Peaceful Change

As in the past, the conflicts and wars that will rage in our future may not be driven so much by religion per se as by economic factors or scarcity of resources, or simply by people looking for a means to power. However, religion will be the most powerful way to galvanize people to action. We have seen this with Hindus and Muslims in India, Catholics and Protestants in the United Kingdom, Muslims and Jews in the

Middle East or Sunnis and Shiites in Iraq. In each case, it is countrymen killing each other in the name of religion. With the continuing march of globalization and its impact on individual identity, it is likely that tomorrow's global leaders will be religious leaders, not political heads of state, and tomorrow's global superpowers will be religions, not nation-states. As such, legitimate leaders of peace-loving religions must recognize this situation as an opportunity to effect positive change in our world and help thwart the efforts of religious fanatics who are using it for their selfish and twisted goals.

> "What is happening with the globaliza-
> tion of religion is a globalization of plu-
> ralism."

Globalization Encourages Religious Pluralism

Peter Berger

Peter Berger is a professor emeritus of religion and sociology at Boston University. In the following viewpoint, Berger claims that globalization is bringing far-flung populations together and fostering a more tolerant global community that encourages religious pluralism. He believes that communication and travel are allowing people to experience different religions and giving them a much greater choice in what faiths to join. This choice of religious affiliation has made most believers more comfortable with their religion and more accepting of all other denominations. In Berger's opinion, only a return to fundamentalism or acquiescence to religious relativism threatens this progressive, middle-ground view of religious tolerance.

As you read, consider the following questions:

1. Why does Berger believe globalization has led to a religious and sociological shift from fate to choice?

Peter Berger, "Religion in a Globalizing World," Pew Forum on Religion & Public Life, December 4, 2006. Reproduced by permission.

2. According to Berger, what have been the consequences of globalizing pluralism on individual beliefs?

3. In what way are relativism and fundamentalism destructive possibilities in a religiously pluralized world, in Berger's opinion?

My thesis is that what is happening with the globalization of religion is a globalization of pluralism. Pluralism, which was a much more geographically, much more limited phenomenon 150 or 200 years ago, has become a global phenomenon, and that has enormous implications, and I want to just draw out these implications. What is pluralism? The term, as far as I know, was coined by Horace Kallen, an American philosopher of the 1920s, whom I think has justly been forgotten. I don't want to be unkind. I once tried to read Kallen and I found him unreadable, but he used the term pluralism in a very normative sense, in a way to celebrate the peaceful coexistence of different ethnic, racial and religious groups in the United States.

Pluralism in the meantime is used in a less value-laden sense to mean simply the fact. Kallen talked about the fact and said it's a good thing. Well, you can use it without the good thing addition, simply as a value-free description of a situation. And I would define pluralism very simply as the coexistence in civic peace—that's very important—of different racial, ethnic and religious groups, with social interaction between them. That, I think, is very important. You can have a plurality of religious groups that do not interact, and then it's a little confusing to talk about pluralism.

Modern Pluralism

I recently was on a panel with a very good Turkish sociologist, and I talked about pluralism—modern pluralism. She said, well, pluralism existed in the Ottoman Empire, the millet system where you had Christians and Jews and various groups being sort of self-contained and given certain rights; that was pluralism. And I said, well, not really, because they didn't interact very much. Or India for example: Many Hindus are very proud of the fact that India has always been pluralistic. Well, there's the caste system, which made it extremely difficult for people to interact. The interaction is important in my concept of pluralism because as people talk to each other, as they converse with each other, they influence each other, and that is the real challenge of pluralism. If I am a member of religious community X and next door there are people from religious community Y, if I don't interact with them and if we agree not to have conflict, it can be a quite tolerable situation, but we're not going to influence each other very much. People influence each other by conversation, and that's a very important element of pluralism.

Now, my proposition is that modern pluralism is different not because it's unique, but because of its global spread and its pervasiveness. There have been pluralistic situations as I defined pluralism in earlier periods of history—very important for the history of Western civilization. The late Roman Empire was pluralistic. Not so incidentally, Christianity came in at that period.

So if you were in metropolitan centers of the Roman Empire—like, let's say, Alexandria—you had a very pluralistic situation. Or in the Book of Acts when the Apostle Paul went to Athens, he found temples and altars to every conceivable god. So that was very pluralistic, and if you look at the literature from that period, it strikes us as very modern. Stay with the example of Alexandria, if you went up the Nile for 50, 60 miles, I think you would come on a world of villagers and towns which were totally non-pluralistic, which were very self-contained. Today it is extremely difficult to find places in the world, which are self-contained in that way. And also the speed with which pluralization occurs today is unique. . . .

From Fate to Choice

Modernity means choices, beginning with many choices in terms of technology. I mean, your tribe used one hammer for a particular task for hundreds of years. Now instead of one hammer, you have three technological systems. And there are choices in terms of consumption, production, marriage, occupation, and, in a sense most dramatically, even identity.

This movement from fate to choice affects not only individuals but also institutions. I would say in the pluralistic situation whether religious institutions like this or not, they become de facto voluntary associations. The prototypical modern, institutional form of religion is the voluntary association. Obviously this voluntariness is enhanced when you have a political and legal system that guarantees religious freedom.

Even if you look at the world today, regimes that try to limit religious freedom—I would say Russia is a good example, China is a good example—of course they suppress the voluntariness, but they can't suppress it completely. And you have all kinds of things springing up, . . . but which the authorities do not like and cannot control.

Another term to use here is the term "denomination," a peculiarly American term. Richard Niebuhr, a church historian—not to be confused with his brother Reinhold—said that denomination was a new form of religious institution peculiar to the United States. And he defined it not as a sect, but a church which recognizes *de facto* [in fact], if not *de jure* [in law], the right of other denominations that do exist. So you can speak of a denominationalization of religion. And take the Roman Catholic Church as a very important example. Certainly it couldn't think of itself as a voluntary association, but it has de facto become one. Probably first in the United States and then after Vatican II, internationally, it has now officially accepted that position with its very impressive doctrine of religious freedom.

Even Judaism: it is not easily understood as a voluntary association with its linkage of religion and ethnicity. In the United States, it has become denominationalized. No matter how you count it, there are at least three Jewish denominations in the United States, and depending on what concept you use, there may be actually five or six.

A Market for Adherents

Now, this leads to very significant changes. It obviously leads to changes in the relationship between religious institutions and the state. It changes the relations of institutions to each other. They become competitors in what in effect is a market, and it changes the relationship of religious institutions and their functions to the laity very significantly. Back to the Roman Catholic example, some Roman Catholic writers in the United States have talked regretfully of the protestantization of American Catholicism. I don't think one should understand this in terms of doctrine. The protestantization is precisely what I'm talking about: the voluntariness of adherence and therefore the importance of the laity. The Catholic laity, certainly in the United States, has become uppity in a way which is very new. I mean, in Boston, where I live, the pluralistic exchange also become players in a religious market.

That's very briefly, I think, the institutional consequences of this globalizing pluralism. There are also very interesting consequences for the individual—again a movement from fate to choice. And increasingly you find individuals who put together their own particular religious profile. You find this very much in North America and in Western Europe. You find it elsewhere as well. Robert Wuthnow, who I think is one of the best sociologists of religion in the United States, has used the term patchwork religion: People put together different elements of their own tradition and other traditions and say, "Well, I'm Catholic, but—." The "but" is very important and there are other things there.

For example, they believe in reincarnation. An enormous number of people in Europe and America believe in reincarnation, which is not exactly Christian doctrine. So that's part of "I'm Catholic, but I believe I've been here many times before," or something like that. Danielle Hervieu-Leger, a French sociologist of religion uses the term "bricolage," which means tinkering. It's like a Lego, you create your own little version of whatever it is you want to call yourself.

The Dangers of Relativism

Now, one topic that I find very important is the interaction of two phenomena, which I would call relativism and fundamentalism. The pluralistic situation inevitably relativizes. If you lose the taken-for-granted status of the tradition, it becomes relativized, and actually our language says this very well. For example, one might say, "I happen to be Catholic"—an extremely interesting phrase. Or a more sort of Californian: "I'm into Buddhism." Which, of course, suggests that tomorrow I might be out of Buddhism, and in fact chances are that I will; I'll discover something else. So there's a relativization that takes place, which is a fact.

Now, relativism I would say is the philosophical legitimization of this fact. It's a good thing, and I suppose the climax of this relativism in religion and in other things is the so-called postmodern theory. We all have our narratives. There's no way of saying that one narrative is superior to another, and the real virtue here is tolerance. We should all tolerate each other's narratives. This, by the way, is fine as long as you deal with religion that is empirically not falsifiable. When you're dealing with morality, this is a recipe for social disintegration. Just take a simple example: You're talking to a victim of rape and you say, well, there's the rapist's narrative and there's your narrative, and you know, you have to respect—well, you can't. If you do that, society will cease to exist. So relativism is a very dangerous direction.

Creating Transnational Ties

Immigrants not only add to the religious diversity of host societies, but also forge connections between societies. These ties emerge organically, but can generally be classified as connections between immigrants and their home country, immigrants and non-immigrants, or immigrants of different countries. Churches become intimately involved in the transnational ties of their congregants, and over time help to institutionalize and routinize these connections. . . .

Besides these direct transnational ties, immigrants interact with other immigrants and with non-immigrants, often in churches. This is one way in which the impact of transnational ties extends beyond immigrant communities into the wider society. In Wuthnow's Global Issues Survey, eight percent of active U.S. church members were immigrants, but 74 percent of members attended congregations in which recent immigrants were present. Qualitative information shows that the presence of immigrants has various effects, both formal and informal, such as initiating special Bible study groups for non-English speakers and spinning off start-up ministries in predominantly immigrant neighborhoods. In addition, the presence of a few recent immigrants sometimes helps in initiating partnerships with churches in other countries and humanitarian programs.

Robert Wuthnow and Stephen Offott,
Sociology of Religion, *2008.*

Fundamentalism can be defined in different ways. I would define it as an attempt to restore or create anew the taken-for-grantedness of a particular worldview, meaning in or of a particular religious tradition, to be taken for granted against a relativization of the modern world. And that's a very difficult project. . . .

In the dialectic between relativism and fundamentalism, looking at it now from the point of view of the healthy society or a healthy democracy, it seems to me both are equally destructive possibilities: relativism because it makes social order in the end impossible; fundamentalism because it creates either civil strife or, at worst when it succeeds, some kind of tyranny. And I think a very important intellectual and indeed political purpose would be to clearly define and occupy the middle ground, which is neither relativistic, in which all questions of truth become obsolete, nor a fundamentalist, militant adherence to absolute truth.

I think that is possible, and I would say in most western countries, most people indeed occupy that middle ground. I think if you look at survey data . . . , you'll find that most Americans are somewhere in the middle on most of the neuralgic [painful] issues of the culture wars. So it's not an impossible project I'm suggesting.

| "The forces of globalization are actually encouraging the proliferation of cultural diversity."

Globalization Promotes Cultural Diversity

Michael Lynton

In the viewpoint that follows, Michael Lynton, the chairman and CEO of Sony Pictures Entertainment, argues that American cultural products—such as movies and television programs—are not dominating global tastes. Instead, Lynton believes that each country favors a mix of local products and imports. This heterogeneity of tastes affects America as well as other nations, forcing Hollywood studios and other image-conscious businesses to market to a culturally diverse audience that has increasingly sophisticated global interests.

As you read, consider the following questions:

1. How does Lynton use theatrical box office returns from Germany, France, India, and Japan to illustrate his point that American imagery is not dominating foreign markets?

Michael Lynton, "Globalization and Cultural Diversity," *Wall Street Journal* vol. 250, September 12, 2007, p. A17. Copyright © 2007 Dow Jones & Company, Inc. All rights reserved. Reprinted with permission of the author.

2. How is Hollywood adapting to the demand for globally diverse films, in the author's opinion?

3. As Lynton explains, where did the concept for the American television program *Ugly Betty* originate?

Is globalization making the world more homogenous? And if so, does Hollywood share the blame?

[In the] summer [of 2007], my studio's [Sony's] *Spider-Man 3* became one of the biggest movies of all time, thanks to its world-wide "web" of box-office success, so it may seem strange for me to say this. But I believe that the global economy in general—and the entertainment business in particular—is absolutely not turning the world into an American shopping mall.

Instead of creating a single, boring global village, the forces of globalization are actually encouraging the proliferation of cultural diversity. Prominent critics like [*New York Times* political and economics columnist] Thomas Friedman disagree. In *The Lexus and the Olive Tree* he argued that globalization "has its own dominant culture, which is why it tends to be homogenizing. . . . Culturally speaking, globalization is largely, though not entirely, the spread of Americanization—from Big Macs to iMacs to Mickey Mouse—on a global scale."

A Balanced Appetite

Yes, it is true that certain products have world-wide reach and appeal. But it is not true that local culture is quashed in the process. Consider that from Germany and France to India and Japan, more than half the theatrical box office is made up of films produced in those lands, in their own languages.

People everywhere like Spider-Man or Disney's Jack Sparrow. A recent Pew poll discovered a "strong appetite" for American cultural exports. But citizens of other countries also like their own heroes and villains, actors and directors. They want to see stories, stars and issues that relate to their own so-

The Diversity of World Music

Despite the American pop juggernaut, music around the world is healthier and more diverse today than ever before. Hardly swamped by output from the multinational conglomerates, local musicians have adapted international influences to their own ends. Most world music styles are of more recent origin than is commonly believed, even in supposedly "traditional" genres: The 20th century brought waves of musical innovation to most cultures, especially the large, open ones. The musical centers of the Third World—Cairo, Lagos, Rio de Janeiro—are heterogeneous and cosmopolitan cities that have welcomed new ideas and new technologies from abroad. Nonetheless, most domestic musical forms have no trouble commanding loyal audiences at home. In India, domestically produced music claims 96 percent of the market; in Egypt, 81 percent; and in Brazil, 73 percent.

Tyler Cowen, Wilson Quarterly, *Autumn 2002.*

cieties and are portrayed and examined in their own languages. That's why, in recent years, we have seen an explosion of creativity from outside Hollywood.

In response to such clear preferences on the part of audiences throughout the world, several major Hollywood studios have created and expanded local-language film production businesses. Our studio is working with directors and actors in China, India, Mexico, Spain and Russia to make movies for release in each of those markets and, on occasion, internationally as well.

That's what we did with Chinese movies like *Crouching Tiger, Hidden Dragon* and *Kung Fu Hustle* which together grossed close to a third of a billion dollars at the world-wide box office. Our first Bollywood film, *Saawariya,* directed by Sanjay Leela Bhansali, [was] released [in] November [2007] in India and throughout the global Indian diaspora.

Adopting and Changing American Television

The same kind of trend is evident with television. When I was growing up in Holland in the late 1960s and 1970s, everyone was watching shows like *The Dukes of Hazzard, Police Woman,* and *Peyton Place.* Nowadays, people there are tuning into home-grown detective shows like *Baantjer* and *Grijpstra & de Gier.*

Today, major Hollywood studios are also involved in making international variations of old American shows such as *The Nanny* and *Married with Children,* adapting the stories to each country's culture and using talent from each land in the starring roles. Sony Pictures is producing original TV series in Chile, Germany, Italy, Russia and Spain.

We're also beginning to see television programs that began somewhere else in the world migrate to America's shores. There's a longer tradition with shows in England being remade in America, such as *All in the Family.* But more recently, we saw *Ugly Betty* become a hit on ABC after it first came out as a Colombian telenovela called *Yo soy Betty, la fea.*

These are not signs of Hollywood's homogenizing effect on the world. They are signs of the world changing the way Hollywood works. It makes sense to marry our production, marketing and distribution experience with the growing global appetite for entertainment tailor-made by and for a variety of cultures.

Heterogeneity Is the Global Trend

So if what can be seen in the cinemas and on television screens from Bangalore to Barcelona these days is any indication, globalization does not mean homogeneity. It means heterogeneity.

Instead of one voice, there are many. Instead of fewer choices, there are more. And instead of a uniform, Americanized world, there remains a rich and dizzying array of cultures, all of them allowing thousands of movies and television shows to bloom.

Audiences around the world are applauding this explosion of home-grown content, because for them, Hollywood is not simply a place in Southern California. It is a symbol of an entertainment culture which is becoming as diverse as it is universal.

"Globalization has [brought] together heterogeneous cultural elements which when mingled are exceedingly volatile."

Globalization Promotes Cultural Antagonism

R.A. Sprinkle

In the following viewpoint, R.A. Sprinkle contends that globalization will likely result in conflict between open societies and closed ones. In Sprinkle's opinion, all nations fear losing sovereignty in a globalized world, but closed societies are most fearful that economic openness will lead to increased outside influence, which in turn might induce their people to rise against state control. While this is a paradox closed societies must face, Sprinkle also believes it will have repercussions for open societies such as the United States. He contends that as these closed, totalitarian nations gain economic strength, they will compete with the United States for resources, and America will find itself either sacrificing its liberal values to continue to trade for needed commodities or contemplating war to keep supply lines open.

As you read, consider the following questions:

1. What does Sprinkle state are the two basic reactions to culture clashes in a globalizing world?

2. How does globalization threaten Islamic cultures, according to Sprinkle?

3. What two emerging powers does Sprinkle believe pose a greater threat to U.S. security and interests than radical Islam?

The object here is not to blame globalization for hostilities between cultures, nor to excuse hostile or malevolent reactions between cultures which are being exacerbated by the convergence of civilizations. The correlation between global conflict and convergence is, however, worthy of consideration, not only to understand the source of tension and global instability today, but also to consider globalization as a catalyst setting off certain forces into an aggressive-defensive mode. It is for this purpose I propose the questions: First, is an increase in terrorism and the radicalization of Islam over the past few decades a reaction to globalization? Furthermore, are many other tensions between nations today related to the transition of nations from self-dependent sovereign states, to a world of interdependent nations converging into a multipolar global society? For the current demand is for international consensus by a majority of nations before action, and nations acting unilaterally in their own defense or best interests are increasingly viewed as pariahs.

While globalization is not the source of Islamic violence—for an inherent nature in certain tenets of Islam has supported violence and suppression from inception—globalization has served as a catalyst by bringing together heterogeneous cultural elements which when mingled are exceedingly volatile. This is in part evidenced by the upsurge in terrorism and increased radicalization of Islam over the past few decades, which corresponds with the global trend towards world socialization.

Fear of Globalization

As nations immerse themselves in modern technologies, global communications, and international commerce, the world transcends further into a global society. With this change all cultures face conflict within as well as without. Societies fear change, not only for the upheaval it may cause, but cultures tend to fear different cultures that are spreading. This discord is particularly evident between tightly controlled collectivist societies vis-à-vis free democratic societies since in some instances ideologies diametrically oppose each other creating suspicions and conflicts.

The current system of nation-states based upon the preservation of national sovereignty, distinct cultures, ideologies and beliefs, has in the past to an extent served to diffuse some conflicts between civilizations by allowing each his own. As global synthesis takes place, however, cultures and ideologies clash resulting in two basic reactions:

The first reaction common in western democracies is to accept diversity, even embrace and promote it. This has resulted in the concept of muliticulturalism where different ideologies, cultures, orientations, and nationalities are all to melt together as one, but yet keep their own group identity. All are granted status as "equals," even if it is felt that special favor and additional advantages need be given to minority groups to make them "equal." At the same time, majorities are often socially demoted in preference to minority or special advocacy groups and actions are taken to sacrifice anything that might inconvenience or offend minority groups, including laws, culture, principles and values.

The other common reaction to globalization is typical of totalitarian societies where freedoms are suppressed. These societies now feel threatened with a loss of power. For while international commerce increases wealth and prosperity, at the same time, dictators, oligarchies, totalitarian regimes, and theo-politicians fear open societies and free markets to the extent it may effect their control by breaking their monopolies of power and the dependency of their people upon them.

There arises therefore, a love-hate relationship with globalization in these totalitarian regimes. For instance, the Saudis embrace and are economically dependent upon the global trade of oil; at the same time they spend vast amounts of their profits to promote Wahabbism [a strongly conservative branch of Islam] which threatens globalization and the oil trade. This seems paradoxical.

The contradiction arises as the result of a clash between interests and ideology, of which, they will surrender neither. They find themselves therefore fighting to retain both. Their ideology is embedded, but on the other hand, it is profitable as well as it is necessary to participate in an evolving world system which they cannot stop, and which also empowers them economically.

For if globalization is inevitable, totalitarians have no intention of melting into one multicultural global society as western elitists imagine to do, but rather, they seek to establish themselves as dominate forces in world affairs in order to preserve their cultures and expand power. The crux of their reaction is, "conquer or be conquered." For while Islamic teachings have always expressed ambitions of global domination, the spread of modern cultural influences and western ideas has created a formidable competitor which they feel threatens their traditions and culture, thus, provoking a violently aggressive-defensive response.

But Islam is not alone in the global struggle for domination; all nations perceive the trend to internationalization and even those anticipating it to varying degrees feel threatened by it. Most do not, however, desire to stop globalization, or if they do, they feel powerless to stop it. It is, therefore, that they seek to be the controlling force behind change in an attempt to mold the shape of things to come. Furthermore, the aspiration to mold the world which is driving Islamic nations is also driving other powers including the US, UK [United Kingdom], EU [European Union], Russia, China, and everyone else who has any global influence. For all are concerned with the final outcome of globalization and wrestle for the greatest degree of power they can obtain in any coming international system.

It was this desire to dominate and compete globally that spawned the creation of the European Union, the modern US-UK alliance, as well as formations of other alliances in the East and Middle East which now reach even unto South America. These alliances are brought about by fear and uncertainty as well as the opportunities created by globalization, and they are motivating forces underlying world tensions today. For even as nations come together, they are fiercely competing one with another and for power.

Multipolarity and Stability

In a 1983 essay on "multipolarity and stability" nuclear strategist Herman Kahn hypothesized that there would arise seven economic giants—the United States, Japan, the Soviet Union, China, Germany, France and Brazil—and that these would eventually work out rules for a world system of order. Although Kahn recognized an inherent stability in the current system of unilateral nation-states where the consequences of nuclear war were so great [that] discipline was the only sane option, he also believed a multipolar system could also be stable, if you could ever get there safely.

The problem was the transition. The moment of maximum danger, Kahn theorized, would occur during the movement of nations from unilateralism to a multipolar world. We are now in that transition, and as Kahn predicted, there are growing tensions and volatilities. For while East and West have both expressed interest in a world order, they are divided by ideological differences, the West, insisting on a universal set of values and human rights as a prerequisite for the foundation of a global society, but the Russians and others holding that common global interests form a sufficient basis upon which to establish a system of international order.

On the other hand, you do have parties who desire no part at all in a world order unless it is based upon absolute submission to their ideology—Enter Islamic extremists.

Globalization threatens the destruction of Islamic culture and beliefs through modernization. Westernization being viewed as a direct attack upon their civilization has created panic and served as an incendiary to ignite many adherents of Islam into action, not only to defend their cultures and beliefs, but to become the supreme power of any coming world order.

As high-minded as this may seem, Islam is but one contender for world supremacy; there is also still the danger of an even greater clash of civilizations between those whose ideologies have Marxist underpinnings and those who hold inalienable rights and freedoms of individuals higher than an arbitrary ruling authority.

Another Struggle

For as the cultural conflict between the West and Islam intensifies, there is another struggle taking place for the control of resources and the global economy. It was for this purpose the European Union was created to be a competitor. Now, however, "former" communist countries have joined the fray having been empowered by the US dollar, open global markets, and a growing share of control of energy supplies.

The opportunity to gain wealth and power has enticed Russia, China, Venezuela, and others to participate in global markets and profits, but, at the same time, they are recoiling internally in an attempt to balance free trade with controlled societies in an effort to achieve both. I would argue that you cannot have both but for the short term, for in the long term the two are incompatible. The only reason closed societies prosper is that they were built by and thrive off of the enterprise of free open societies, but this is temporal; they cannot sustain themselves. However, as these totalitarian societies are empowered economically, they will struggle with and eventually unite to supersede the free nations from which they have derived their wealth and power.

On the other hand, the nation which has empowered totalitarian governments the most in an effort to establish a new world order has been the United States. No nation has done more to bring it into being, nor has it been done without design or manipulation of politicians and financial powers, for it has been contemplated, planned, and worked toward for decades. Unfortunately, the ideology driving the establishment of free trade with totalitarian nations was built upon the misconception that globalization and free trade by themselves would eventually break down barriers and bring about a global democracy. . . .

Sacrificing Principles for Profits

For decades elitist drones have realized the power and wealth that could be created through globalization and have set about to establish international controls to make it feasible. In so doing they have discounted the importance of individual freedoms and moral principles essential to the foundation and stability of any free system—for although you can have stability in a system absent a foundation comprised of these, it requires totalitarianism. When the overriding goal of government is to achieve peace, stability and the unity of nations at any price, at the end of the road is either war against, or surrender to a tyranny.

The West's Air of Superiority

The West generally judges the merits of human societies in terms of material wealth and power, taken to be the products of enlightened progress. We Westerners believe that we now are creating, as *New York Times* writer Roger Cohen recently put it, "a century that will make a diverse world more unified, prosperous, and free than ever before."

Both liberals and conservatives in modern Western society firmly believe that. Since Europe's exploration of Asia and the Americas, which predated the West's technological advantage over Asian societies, and which awakened Christian zeal to convert those peoples, the West has increasingly regarded itself as superior to the rest and the bearer of truth. It seems inconceivable to most Westerners that the traditional world, in which everyone except themselves lives, might remain a coherent and valid cultural system for those who live in it. The issue does not even arise as to whether a backward culture—by our standards—could progress in its own terms so as to merit respect for its autonomous qualities.

William Pfaff,
Commonweal, *June 16, 2006.*

Because the United States opened the door to prosperity for other nations whose values are contrary, these nations, many of them totalitarian, are now becoming powerful enough, if not alone then confederated one with another, to challenge the US on many fronts. Thus, by empowering these totalitarian states, the US became a global prostitute who agreed to "put out" now for payment later and is now in jeopardy having already put out.

If the US should reject many aspects of a global system proposed by the totalitarian parties it has empowered, US dependency for oil and goods is so great it faces isolation and the possibility of future military conflict. If, however, the US capitulates and agrees to a system that is based upon common interests rather than values, as these nations gain enough leverage they will be able to manipulate the US diplomatically, or collapse the US economically—this is already occurring to a degree as is evident in the capitulation of US foreign policy internationally. It is unwise to focus upon the threat of radical Islam while ignoring such emerging powers as Russia and China, which pose a greater threat. Islamic nations would have little wherewithal without any support from more modernized powers.

If America, as Abraham Lincoln stated, is the "best last hope of mankind" it will only be so by the underlying principles which made America. Forsaking or compromising those principles in order to create a multicultural global society for the "common good" will produce a corrupt global hive indeed. For the eventual result of a world order built on shared interests alone will be the loss of liberty, global conflict, and, eventually, total breakdown and chaos—for interests and loyalties shift, sound principles do not.

Now consider a parable: In 1956 Brazilian scientists were attempting to create a new hybrid bee in the hopes of creating improved honey production when African bees were accidentally introduced into the wild in the Americas. The new hybrid, known as the "Africanized" or "killer bee," took many years to establish colonies; as it did, it began to radicalize, taking over and corrupting the hives of domestic bees. This Africanized bee is extremely aggressive-defensive, easily agitated by anything deemed foreign, and it produces little honey. Thus, the result is that it is unprofitable for the keeper and a threat to all others.

> "Globalization certainly will produce many winners, but . . . some of the disgruntled losers might lead successful revolts against modernization."

Globalization Could Result in a Backlash Against Modernity

James W. Thomson

James W. Thomson is a writer and owner of an investment firm in Washington State. He claims in the following viewpoint that the drive toward modernization brought on by free trade is not welcomed in all developing nations. Though supposedly a means to bring about political as well as economic change, globalization can divide populations along racial, ethnic, and class lines, Thomson argues, if privileged elites benefit when the masses do not. According to Thomson, antiglobalization movements are springing up to question the social divisiveness of such unrestrained capitalism. If powerful enough, these movements might disrupt the free trade system and, coupled with protectionist measures already in place by developed nations, undermine any intended positive effects of globalization.

James W. Thomson, "Consequences of Globalization," *USA Today*, vol. 137, September 2008, pp. 72–74. Copyright © 2008 Society for the Advancement of Education. Reproduced by permission.

As you read, consider the following questions:

1. According to Thomson, what does Amy Chua believe is a good remedy for economic imbalance in developing countries, and why does Thomson see shortcomings in this solution?

2. In the author's view, what two things have influenced many American economists in reconsidering the effects of free-market-style globalization?

3. What led to the rise of populist anti-immigrant movements in the nineteenth century, according to Thomson?

For many skeptics, globalization merely is a transparent euphemism for "Americanization," the global diaspora of American-style capitalism and, with it, the spread of its materialistic values. At best, our culture can be exciting and, sometimes, perhaps liberating. Yet, what often is perceived is the worst that we have to offer—from the narcissism of the Shopping Channel to the macho posturing of steroid-fueled TV wrestlers. For the left (and for many moderates and conservatives as well), globalization widely is perceived as a means by which the U.S. can expand its global influence under the more attractive banner of modernization. Although globalization is grounded upon economic activities, it has significant political and social ramifications: clearly, it cannot exist without political pre-conditions; conversely, it may be derailed by political "backlash" as symbolized by the impact of antiglobalization protests.

Defenders of Globalization

Most advocates of worldwide trade, such as economist Jeffrey D. Sachs, author of *The End of Poverty*, believe that free markets and democratic political institutions could eliminate poverty in the Third World by transforming those nations into a community of peaceful and prosperous societies. However, this hope just may prove to be a tempting illusion since globalization advocates also tend to believe that ethnic hatreds, sectarian bitterness, and other forms of social backwardness would be swept away by modernization. As a cautionary tale, the current sectarian struggle for political supremacy in Iraq should be a painful wakeup call for many such true believers. Nonetheless, the globalization movement still has numerous enthusiastic supporters. Among the best-known is *New York Times* columnist Thomas Friedman, author of *The Lexus and the Olive Tree* and *The World Is Flat*. Both books express exceedingly high expectations for globalization. For Friedman, globalization tends to turn all friends and enemies into competitors, with the result being multiethnic, pluralistic, free-market democracies. Optimism aside, two issues remain; will the values that our elites favor for the U.S. find acceptance abroad? Moreover, will they even work in this country?

In a seminal essay, "World on Fire," drawn from her book of the same title, Amy Chua, a Chinese-American economist and law professor at Yale University, asserts that the global spread of capitalism and democracy has certain potential dangers. In recent decades, according to Chua, emerging populist and democratic movements in the developing world have provided appealing legitimacy for the impoverished masses—precisely those who likely would be the most susceptible to anti-American demagoguery. Chua has argued that free elections inevitably would result in the rise to power of many anticapitalist and American political leaders. Since her book was published [in 2003], Chua's fears have been realized by the turbulent political events in Venezuela, Ecuador, Peru, and Bolivia, as well as the ill-fated consequences of the U.S. involvement in Iraq. Nonetheless, for decades, U.S. policymakers consistently have advocated free markets and democracy as politico-economic elixirs for establishing peace and prosperity for developing countries as well as the post-Communist nations of Eastern Europe without reckoning all the consequences carefully.

"Anti-Globalization," cartoon by Kjell Nilsson-Maki. www.CartoonStock.com.

The Backlash

As a specialist on developing countries, Chua points out that much of the ongoing debate over globalizaton in the West has been focused on the familiar left-wing notions of class conflict and the exploitation of workers while neglecting the more complex ethnic and racial dimensions. Although the left-liberal approach might make some sense for Western societies, it is inadequate for certain developing nations where economic life long has been driven by "market-dominant" minorities such as the Chinese in the Philippines (including Chua's family). The author has provided a lengthy list of examples: the Chinese in Indonesia, Myanmar, and Malaysia; whites in Latin America and sub-Saharan Africa; Israelis in the Middle East; ethnic Russians in Central Asia; the Ibos of Nigeria; the Serbs and Croats in the former Yugoslavia; and the Jews in post-Communist Russia. In recent years, these minority groups have been subject to unrest and violence. Chua believes that populist movements in developing nations might lead to backlash policies aimed at these dominant minorities that could take three possible forms: a rejection of free markets and capitalism, attacks on democracy, and violence directed against these groups. The most chilling parallel to Chua's thesis is the tragic fate of European Jewry, who had formed an extraordinarily successful dominant minority group for centuries prior to the Holocaust.

Globalization can result in drastic political and economic transformations that can uproot entire societies. The bloody legacy of Europe during the last century is the best reminder of the hazards of radical economic and political transformations. If globalization results in economic changes that benefit some ethnic or racial groups more than others, then a powerful backlash against it easily could occur—not only in poor countries, but in developed nations.

As possible remedies, Chua proposes using "affirmative action" programs for developing countries. However, she fails to acknowledge that such racially-based policies quickly can polarize entire societies. In Cuba, the dominant white business class fled shortly after Fidel Castro declared his intentions to eliminate their economic and political power. In South Africa, many highly educated whites have abandoned their homeland of three centuries after the black majority South African government announced similar plans. In Brazil, the jury remains out and uneasy after its popular left-wing president, Lula da Silva, proposed sweeping race-oriented affirmative action plans. In many Western nations, nonwhites now comprise a significant portion of the population while certain racial groups, such as Asians and East Indians in the U.S., for instance, are significantly wealthier than the average white American. In general, affirmative action programs provide substantial privileges on the basis of race, ethnicity, and gender. Consequently, right-wing populists such as [columnist and commentator] Patrick Buchanan can argue persuasively that American politics has degenerated into virtual tribal warfare waged between the winners and losers of affirmative action initiatives and other redistribution schemes championed by left-liberals.

The Harsh Reality

Although the debate over globalization, led by the likes of Chua and Columbia University's Jagdish Bhagwati and Joseph Stiglitz (the latter the 2001 Nobel Prize winner in Economics), among many others, may sound like a heated debate at a faculty seminar, the international stakes are much higher. Today, more than half of the students in U.S. universities working toward advanced degrees in economics are foreign-born; most are wealthy and well-connected; and many eventually will return home to pursue careers in government, business, and academia.

During the 1980s, there was a widespread consensus among American economists that the liberalization of trade and financial markets would prove to be beneficial for developing economies. Many foreign students from U.S. universities returned home to advocate what they had heard in their classrooms—capitalism had worked well and socialism had failed; globalization would work wonders because it would make good use of the liberating effects of free markets. Today, things are quite different. Following the Asian financial crisis of the late 1990s and the various structural problems that plagued many post-Communist countries in their attempts to modernize, along with the lagging economic growth of many developing economies, a significant number of influential American economists have begun to reconsider the effect of free-market-style globalization.

In his classes, Stiglitz has stated, "Capitalism, American-style, has some real problems." In *Globalization and Its Discontents*, he contends that globalization still could enrich people everywhere but, in practice, it often has damaged the economies of developing nations. Furthermore, he claims that globalization could work only if the International Monetary Fund was less aggressive in pressuring developing nations to open their markets to free trade and if these countries would focus more on creating "safety nets" to cushion their own citizens from the economic "shocks" of globalization. Stiglitz is more concerned about the social and political dimensions of the process, and places greater emphasis on creating effective political and social institutions rather than simply relying upon powerful market forces to transform societies.

As for free trade, he believes it could work if it were implemented by all nations. However, he maintains that it has not been used fairly by advanced economies, as many of them have resorted to protectionist measures.

At Harvard University, Dani Rodrik has written a series of articles and books addressing globalization. He analyzes the varied social and political issues that many developing nations have encountered in their attempts to modernize their economies. Like Sachs and Stiglitz, Rodrik believes that the political and social aspects of globalization often have been overlooked in favor of the stringent free-market policies advocated by the U.S., International Monetary Fund, and World Bank. However, remaining unconvinced is Bhagwati, a proponent of free trade. He says that globalization and foreign investment have proven quite beneficial for developing countries, particularly India and China, and that both of these factors drastically have improved the economic status of hundreds of millions of people, particularly women.

The Underside of Globalization

Globalization advocates often insist that the success of this movement is inevitable, but history provides a very different perspective. In the past, many highly developed societies have collapsed, but none more surprisingly than the demise of the former Soviet Union. According to Harold James, economic historian and author of *The End of Globalization*, a more striking example is the failure of the first attempt at globalization, which lasted for roughly 100 years—from 1815 (the year of Napoleon's defeat at Waterloo) to 1914 (the outbreak of World War I). By the end of the 19th century, the global economy was integrated through the almost unhindered mobility of goods, capital flows, and people. Foreign trade was relatively tariff-free; production quotas were unknown; passports were not required; borders were unguarded; and immigration was unchecked. In search of prosperity, millions of Europeans and Asians left their homelands to seek out better opportunities in the New World. The countries receiving these immigrants usually enjoyed substantial economic growth while the natives of the receiving countries often were affected negatively. Often, the reduced earnings of native workers led to populist anti-immigrant political action such as the American Know Nothing movement of the 1850s. European countries— such as Ireland, Italy, and Poland—sending these immigrants soon realized productivity gains coupled with sizable increases in personal incomes that allowed these then-undeveloped European nations to escape from poverty.

Free Trade in Free Fall

After the bloodbath of World War I, many of the political and economic institutions that previously had aided globalization quickly were eliminated in one country after another. High tariffs become the norm, bringing to an end almost a century of free trade. The U.S. led the way with the ill-fated Smoot-Hawley Act of 1930. Immigration, especially from Europe, drastically was curtailed by restrictive laws passed during the 1920s. The world's central bankers eventually turned to market intervention policies to regulate international capital flows and the values of their domestic currencies.

Finally, monetary instability in many countries, particularly in Germany and the U.S., plus the political crises associated with the divisive issues of war reparation payments ended with the virtual breakdown of the global economy during the interwar years. By the late 1930s, many influential Western government officials, economists, and businessmen reluctantly had concluded that global economic integration no longer was feasible and that their future policy hopes should be based upon effective and timely government intervention. At the depths of the Great Depression in 1933, English economist John Maynard Keynes famously declared, "Let goods be home-spun whenever it is reasonably and conveniently possible and, above all, let finance be primarily national." This pessimistic conjecture marked a complete departure from the classic liberal economic doctrine, with its faith in the gains to be realized by all nations from free trade.

It turned out that the political solutions for the crises of global capitalism during the Depression usually proved worse than the world economic meltdown. All too often, the shift from capitalism led to political dictatorships in Germany, Russia, Spain, and Italy—to name just a few—and to mostly ineffectual government intervention in many of the world's democratic societies, including the U.S. and Great Britain. By the outbreak of World War II, the liberal democratic nations of the West had been discredited by their failed economic policies and their lack of political resolve.

During the bleak 1930s, Adolf Hitler's Third Reich claimed economic miracles of rapid economic growth while the rest of the world suffered through the Great Depression. In the Soviet Union, Joseph Stalin's Communist propagandists made similar economic claims that succeeded in bamboozling many observers, particularly left-wing Western intellectuals, such as [economist] John K. Galbraith, well into the 1980s. After the apparent triumphs of authoritarian rule in Europe during the Depression years, a number of those nations' economic policies were emulated in the U.S. (including some from Benito Mussolini's Fascist Party in Italy) as part of Franklin Roosevelt's New Deal agenda. In retrospect, most of these latter policies proved to be quite unwise. Eventually, the full truth became known, but not until 1945 for the democratic Nazi regime. Meanwhile, the massive blunders of CCCP [Soviet]-style communism were not completely exposed until after the meltdown of the Soviet Union by 1991.

Winners and Losers

The current backlash against globalization stems primarily from a number of linked political and social issues. Clearly, globalization does represent a serious challenge for privileged elites, whether they exercise control of an advanced economy, such as France or Japan, or if they wield power in a developing nation, such as Brazil, South Korea, or Saudi Arabia. Adding to the turbulent political mix, globalization certainly will produce many winners, but it will propagate losers as well— and there is a very good chance that some of the disgruntled losers might lead successful revolts against modernization.

In this presidential election year [2008], the Democrats especially have been noisy on the issues of globalization and free trade, favoring instead what has been labeled "The Third Way" by former Pres. Bill Clinton and Tony Blair, Britain's ex-prime minister. Should globalization indeed lead to fragmentation and decline, as it did in the 1930s, it would be, in the words of baseball "linguist" Yogi Berra, "Déjà vu all over again"—and that would not be a good thing.

Periodical Bibliography

The following articles have been selected to supplement the diverse views presented in this chapter.

Benjamin R. Barber   "Shrunken Sovereign Consumerism, Globalization, and American Emptiness," *World Affairs*, Spring 2008.

Peter Berger   "Faith and Development," *Society*, January 2009.

Robert Chrisman   "Globalization and the Media Industry," *Black Scholar*, Summer/Fall 2008.

Barry K. Gills   "The End of the War on Terror," *Globalizations*, March 2009.

Michael Goodhart   "Human Rights and Global Democracy," *Ethics and International Affairs*, Winter 2008.

Teresa Lesher   "Globalization and Islam," *I-Mag*, Summer 2007.

William Morehouse   "Globalization on Steroids," *American Scholar*, Winter 2009.

Richard Pells   "Does the World Still Care About American Culture?" *Chronicle of Higher Education*, March 6, 2009.

Robert B. Reich   "How Capitalism Is Killing Democracy," *Foreign Policy*, September/October 2007.

Majid Tehranian   "Globalization and Religious Resurgence: An Historical Perspective," *Muslim World*, July 2007.

CHAPTER 2

What Is Globalization's Impact on World Crises?

Chapter Preface

The globalization of economic markets typically requires that products be shipped from one nation to another—often from one continent to another. To make this global trade work, freight handlers need fuel to supply the fleets of planes, ships, and trucks that transport the goods from factory to market. But high oil prices—which in part have been driven upward by unbridled global trade—are challenging the continuance of globalization. Lois Parshley, writing for Global Envision, a promoter of open markets, states simply, "Higher prices are upsetting the global supply chains that until now considered cheap labor and raw materials more important than geography."

For American companies, Parshley reports, the spike in oil prices has prompted some to reconsider geography. While communications and Internet technologies—services that deal with products that can be transmitted instead of shipped—will likely remain in whatever distant land can do the work cheaply, manufacturing will experience the greatest shake-up. Corporations that outsource manufacturing to China, for example, may look again at the benefits of moving production to Mexico. Yet if China loses some American markets, it may gain new markets in neighboring states. As Dan Steinbock, research director of International Business at the India, China and America Institute, writes in a 2008 issue of *China Daily*, "If the cost of moving things and people continues to soar, globalization will erode and regionalization will gain." That is, countries may expand trade with others in their region, reshaping globalization into a series of regional partnerships.

Some believe the retrenchment of globalization may prove beneficial. In the United States, the steel industry, which has been in decline due to competition from abroad, is witnessing a boost as the cost of importing steel from China is rising. Indeed, China's steel export to the United States dropped 20 percent in 2008, leaving Pittsburgh and other steel towns to pick up the slack. But energy is still the key, and no matter where the United States obtains consumer goods, it will need oil to transport them to market. This fact has left many observers warning that access to oil reserves will be important for both energy security and economic security.

In the chapter that follows, analysts and commentators examine some of the worldwide crises that are influenced by expanded global free trade. Many blame globalization for exacerbating problems associated with everything from financial markets to the environment. In their opinion, the pursuit of profit has blinded global corporations to the costs of unrestricted trade. Globalization's defenders, however, contend that bringing nations together through trade will also help them perceive global crises as a shared responsibility that might be resolved by strengthening international bonds. In the same way that high oil prices might provide perks to regional markets, globalization, according to its advocates, may provide unanticipated answers to national as well as worldwide problems.

> *"Globalization of the Clinton-Bush era not only lacked safeguards for labor but rested on two mutually reinforcing, flawed models of growth."*

Mismanaged Globalization Is Responsible for the Modern Financial Crisis

Sherle R. Schwenninger

In the viewpoint that follows, Sherle R. Schwenninger argues that globalization helped bring about the 2008 world financial crisis by encouraging debt-financed consumption in Western nations and by not prompting Asian nations to balance their savings and production trends. In Schwenninger's opinion, the West took advantage of low-wage labor in developing nations, bringing about a loss of manufacturing in the West and a higher demand for energy in the East. In the United States, this raised gas prices while more and more people were losing jobs to overseas firms. With less disposable income, consumers could not afford to keep up their consumption and markets began to decline. In Asian economies like China, the massive demand for products led to more profits, but wages remained low, Schwenninger main-

Sherle R. Schwenninger, "Redoing Globalization," *Nation*, vol. 288, January 12–19, 2009, pp. 30–32. Copyright © 2009 by The Nation Magazine/The Nation Company, Inc. Reproduced by permission.

tains. Consequently, consumer spending could not rise to keep the economy moving forward. Schwenninger believes the U.S. government will have to strengthen its diplomatic bargaining to bring various nations together to rectify globalization's shortcomings. Sherle R. Schwenninger is the director of the economic growth program at the New America Foundation, a nonprofit public policy organization.

As you read, consider the following questions:

1. In Schwenninger's view, what was the root cause of the unbalanced world economy that led to the crisis?

2. What does the author believe the Obama administration should ask of China that would strike a "positive" note in redressing the global crisis?

3. Why does Schwenninger believe it is important for nations to fund the International Monetary Fund and World Bank during the financial crisis?

The great financial bubble of the [Bill] Clinton-[George W.] Bush years has ended in tears—in home foreclosures, bank failures and what promises to be the most severe global economic recession since the Great Depression. As President-elect [Barack] Obama puts together his economic recovery program, he needs to understand that the economic crisis is the result not just of unscrupulous mortgage lenders and unregulated investment bankers on Wall Street but of the globalization of finance and trade that key members of his economic team set in motion when they were in the Clinton administration. The uncomfortable truth is that the current system of global commerce and transnational finance is inherently prone to crisis and is incompatible with Obama's goal of rebuilding the American middle class. Any sustainable recovery on the domestic front, therefore, will depend on his success in getting other countries to agree to fundamental changes in that global system.

Globalization Without Safeguards

Globalization is not necessarily bad if properly regulated among similar economies. But the globalization of the Clinton-Bush era not only lacked safeguards for labor but rested on two mutually reinforcing, flawed models of growth: debt-financed consumption in the United States and other Anglo-Saxon economies and oversaving and underconsumption in the production-oriented export economies of Asia. Not surprisingly, the global integration of these radically different economies produced an unhealthy pattern of growth characterized by asset bubbles and large global trade imbalances, with the United States running large deficits and China and Japan running large surpluses.

The root cause of this unbalanced world economy was the enormous pool of excess savings generated by China, Japan and, more recently, the petrodollar states of the Persian Gulf. This global savings glut, as Federal Reserve chair Ben Bernanke called it, helped fuel a succession of asset bubbles in the United States, culminating in the expansion of easy credit and the rapid run-up of housing prices following the collapse of the tech-stock bubble. The housing and credit bubble in turn helped inflate consumption by enabling households to take on more debt; household debt as a percentage of disposable income rose from 90 percent in the late 1990s to 133 percent in 2007.

This pattern of economic growth had other worrying features. Corporate profits soared as companies in the developed world took advantage of China's low wages, lax environmental standards and undervalued currency to locate production there. But wages and family income in the United States stagnated under this and other low-wage competition (as well as from the declining power of organized labor). As a result, income and wealth inequality increased in the United States and China. The US tradable-goods sector also took a hit as Japan, China and other Asian economies manipulated their currencies to maintain competitive advantage. [From 2001 to 2008] the United States lost nearly 4 million manufacturing jobs. During this same period, large chunks of industrial capacity were transferred from more energy-efficient developed countries to energy-inefficient developing countries like China, which compensated for its energy inefficiency with lower wages. This relocation of production helped spur increased demand for oil and gas, setting off an energy price spiral, which was exacerbated by bubblelike speculation in these commodities. Higher oil prices resulted in the transfer of huge amounts of wealth from middle- and working-class people in the United States and other oil-importing countries to oil producers in the Gulf and elsewhere.

This pattern of economic growth was not sustainable because it caused a huge shortfall in global demand, which had to be filled by America's debt-financed consumption—the US current-account (all the goods and services imported balanced against those exported) deficit increased from 1.7 percent of GDP [gross domestic product] in 1997 to 6.5 percent a decade later. Economic growth came to a crashing halt when US households reached the point where they could no longer take on more debt. The bursting of the housing and credit bubble set off a deleveraging process that has spread across the world economy. In fact, few countries have been immune to falling asset prices and frozen credit markets, or to rapidly falling demand for their goods and services.

Surplus Economics Spur Global Demand

Because the incoming Obama administration faces a crisis of global proportions, a recovery program will have to be global in scope, and it will have to correct the huge imbalances globalization created. The president-elect has said very little about his international economic policy. But if he wants to see a sustained recovery, he will have to put forth an international economic reform program that is as bold as his proposed domestic program. The reason is simple: given the high levels of household debt, the US economy can no longer be the demand locomotive that pulls the rest of the world out of recession. Other economies will have to pull alongside the US economy.

The main focus of the new administration's international economic statecraft must be on the large current-account surplus economies—China, Japan, Germany and the petrodollar states, which are running surpluses of 9.5 percent, 4 percent, 7.3 percent and more than 10 percent, respectively. These economies must lead in spurring world growth not only because, with the United States, they bear responsibility for the crisis but also because they are in the best position to lead, given their large surpluses and foreign currency. For better or worse, they must become the collective substitute for the American locomotive, either by stimulating demand in their own economies or by recycling their surpluses to stimulate demand in other economies.

The first element of the new administration's global program should be to encourage China and other large surplus economies to expand domestic demand to offset weakened US consumption. Germany, Japan and the Gulf states are well positioned to expand their economies—preferably by cutting taxes on consumption and increasing social spending to spur more domestic consumption. China has announced what at first appeared to be an impressive stimulus program of $586 billion over two years. But it turned out to be mostly a repackaging of existing spending commitments by local governments and state companies and was heavily weighted toward infrastructure investment, which in the case of China will do little to create domestic consumer demand. Worse, the central government took steps to shore up the export economy by increasing export subsidies and allowing the yuan to depreciate, thus making Chinese goods less expensive in the world market.

In shoring up its exports as well as its state-led investment sectors, China has embraced what amounts to a beggar-thy-neighbor strategy that supports its growth by taking a larger share of a shrinking global pie. And that is what global depressions are made of. A change in the pattern of China's growth is not only critical but long overdue. Over the past decade, investment and savings there have grown much faster than consumption. Consequently, China has an unusually high savings rate of nearly 50 percent, while consumption constitutes only 35 percent of the economy. A world economy simply cannot function when the second-largest economy (measured by purchasing-power parity) has such a lopsided imbalance between savings and consumption.

Enticing China to Act

The Obama administration therefore needs to signal to Beijing that it is unacceptable for China to run such large surpluses and that it urgently needs to do more to generate consumer demand. The new administration must make clear that if Beijing does not do more to support a global recovery, Washington will be forced to radically reshape its trading relationship with China when the crisis is over.

The first appeal to China, however, should be to its own interests as well as to its expressed desire to be a responsible stakeholder in the global economy. Indeed, the overarching message of Obama's international statecraft should be strikingly positive: the United States is not demanding austerity and painful budget cuts, as the Clinton administration did of so many East Asian countries after the 1997–98 crisis. It is asking China to raise the living standards of its workers, spend more on their healthcare and education, and provide a decent pension for older citizens. These things should endear China's leaders to their people and lessen the risk of internal social conflict. . . .

Obama also needs to make it clear that the reason the United States is pressing China and other Asian economies to raise wages and improve living standards is not so it can reclaim jobs lost to China but to increase global demand so *all* economies can create more jobs. Higher wages in China and other high-savings Asian economies would increase the purchasing power of Asian workers and augment consumer demand. The US economy would indirectly benefit from those higher wages and living standards because it would increase the demand for US goods and services, especially for labor-saving and efficiency-enhancing technology.

The quickest way for China to raise its living standards is by increasing the value of the yuan against the dollar and other international currencies. A stronger yuan would stem future inflation while reducing the cost of food, energy and other imports for Chinese consumers. Appreciating the value of the yuan would be a first step in a broader realignment of world currencies to help correct global trade imbalances. . . .

A World Economic Recovery Fund

Some of the surplus economies will not be able to stimulate consumer demand sufficiently in the short term to reduce their surpluses to acceptable levels. That leaves the alternative—recycle some of those surpluses to stimulate growth and economic development in other countries. The United States, of course, will need access to some of these surpluses to help fund its recovery program, but other surpluses could be redirected to support what should be a second pillar of the new administration's world economic recovery plan—namely, establishing a world economic recovery fund to deal with balance-of-payments crises and to support public works projects in developing economies.

A number of countries—Iceland, Hungary, Pakistan and Ukraine—have suffered serious debt and liquidity problems related to the crisis and have sought money from the International Monetary Fund [IMF] and other sources. These countries may need more money in the months ahead, while countries in Eastern Europe, Africa, Asia and Latin America may also experience currency-related crises before the world economy is stabilized. The IMF, however, has only $250 billion for managing national debt crises—a mere pittance compared with the rescue plans that the United States, Britain and other G-20 [an international economic forum] governments have embarked on or those that are needed to deal with the approaching crises in Turkey, the Baltic states and elsewhere.

It is therefore important to shore up the IMF and the World Bank, quickly. The IMF could be a helpful stabilizer in global financial markets if it had access to the sizable reserves of the surplus economies and if it pursued a philosophy more in keeping with the original Keynesian vision of those Bretton Woods organizations [the 1944 conference of nations that sought monetary stability and increased global economic exchange and that followed the economic theories of John Maynard Keynes]. To make this change possible, the Obama administration should offer the surplus economies a new Bretton Woods grand bargain: in return for making outsize contributions to the world economic recovery fund from which the IMF and the World Bank could draw working capital, the United States would support giving these countries a greater say in the running of the IMF and the World Bank.

Previous US administrations blocked efforts to increase the working capital of the IMF and the World Bank because the proposed measures threatened Washington's pre-eminent position in these institutions—as well as its de facto veto, since increasing the allocations of Japan, Germany and other surplus economies in the G-20 would have increased their weighted vote. That has turned out to be shortsighted, because we have been left with cash-strapped and ineffective international institutions. That has put more burden on the Federal Reserve to use US monetary policy as a world crisis

Bank Asset Losses and Capital Gains, 2008

Figures are in billions of dollars.

	Loss	Capital	Difference
Worldwide	507.4	361.4	−146.0
Americas	254.6	184.0	−70.6
Europe	228.8	155.4	−73.4
Asia	24.0	22.0	−2.0

TAKEN FROM: Rebecca Wilder, "G7 Supports the U.S. Bailout of Asset-Backed Securities... Duh!" News N Economics, September 22, 2008. www.newsneconomics.com.

stabilizer, which contributed to the buildup of the large asset bubbles of the past decade. It has also left the door open for the big surplus economies to use their sovereign wealth funds to influence the course of world capital markets.

Stabilizing the Global Economy

An emergency world economic recovery fund would enable the IMF and the World Bank, along with regional development banks, to carry out a global macroeconomic stimulus program to supplement national fiscal expansion. The IMF could tap the fund to carry out currency stabilization programs and help countries manage balance-of-payments problems. The World Bank and regional development banks could tap the fund to accelerate lending for job-creating public works and social investment in developing countries. Fund money could also be made available to UN projects related to healthcare, education, nutrition and the environment. This increased social and public spending would help stabilize consumption and investment in vulnerable developing and emerging economies, and aid a global economic recovery.

The underlying rationale of such a global stimulus program is that it would be more effective and less potentially inflationary over the longer term than a solely domestic fiscal expansion. Just as important, such a world public-sector program, together with a new system of managing world currencies, would point the way to the institutional reform needed to correct the many failings of the globalization of the Clinton-Bush era.

> *"Globalisation will keep transmitting the shocks along with the benefits unless we . . . strengthen the multilateral instruments that govern the global financial system."*

A Better-Regulated Globalization Can Limit the Modern Financial Crisis

Peter Mandelson

In the following viewpoint, Peter Mandelson argues that globalization needs an oversight body that would regulate trade and reduce excessive risk-taking in financial markets. If such an organization was empowered to monitor globalization, then the benefits of expanded free trade could limit the extent of the crisis. Peter Mandelson served as the European commissioner for trade from 2004 to 2008, when he was made business secretary in the cabinet of British prime minister Gordon Brown.

As you read, consider the following questions:

1. Why does Mandelson say that politicians need to recognize that national solutions to the crisis are not enough?

2. Why does the author contend that it is a mistake to believe that globalization puts governments out of business?

3. What are the three things that the author claims politicians and economists will learn from the financial crisis?

We will look back on the banking crisis of September 2008 as a defining moment for economic globalisation. It may have started in the US mortgage market and on Wall Street, but through an integrated global economy it has become an international problem. Whatever our response, we should be guided by two principles. First, we should not jettison our commitment to globalisation. Second, a global economy needs global governance.

Globalisation works by widening economic networks. It multiplies the sizes of markets, increases the economies of scale that push down prices, and allows countries to tap into sources of productive investment from around the world. Those networks have created a global economic engine that is the biggest eliminator of poverty and creator of opportunity the world has ever seen. But globalisation transmits risk and volatility as well as benefits.

Sustaining the huge benefits of economic globalisation relies on preserving these fundamental networks of interdependence, not rolling them back. Changes to financial regulatory frameworks must tackle excessive risk while defending open trade and foreign investment as vital to development.

Regulating Risk Taking

Beyond ending the liquidity crisis, our first response should be to fix the source of the shock. We need to inject confidence by regulating to control excessive risk-taking and heavy leveraging, and to improve the way ratings agencies work. The European commission is right to now come forward with new European rules on these questions. Certain financial products have become so complex that they are not understood by the very institutions that buy and trade them. This is a regulatory and professional failure of the first order.

Politicians need to recognise that national solutions are only half the solution. For years, financial markets have been global more than national, yet they operate with limited multilateral coordination or governance. Asset bubbles in one market can have serious consequences in another. The effects of monetary or currency policy are easily exported. Yet the machinery of global economic governance barely exists.

Mechanisms for cross-border cooperation in Europe exist but they are incomplete. The rescue package for Dutch financial group Fortis showed European governments can act quickly to limit damage. But the Benelux states [Belgium, the Netherlands, and Luxembourg] that stepped in to help the group have close ties and habits of cooperation. Guarantees for Irish banks have proved more politically complex. The general mechanisms of European coordination must be strengthened so governments and regulators act effectively to address the fact that many financial institutions operate across borders.

The Need for Oversight

Internationally, the problem is even more acute. There is no institution with a mandate or real capacity to assess systemic risk in financial markets. There is no institution empowered to speak from the perspective of global economic interdependence and to counsel states on the global picture. Coordination mechanisms among central bankers and regulators exist, but they are weak.

They are also skewed towards an economic order that is increasingly outdated. The large emerging economies—especially China—are growing sources of capital and economic demand. They are tightly knit into the global economy. Bodies like the G8 [group of eight most economically strong devel-

Globalization Intensified

It is obvious that the fall-out of the [2008] U.S. financial crisis, not only in the U.S., but throughout the world will be enormous and unfathomable for months to come as the debris is sorted out.

But one effect already seems to be clear and far-reaching: the crisis and its implications for the world outside the U.S. already indicate that the pace of globalization will be given a further spurt. It will lead to a whole new plateau of intensified relationships on the economic, and therefore, the political plane among the world players.

The bonds that have been forged in the post-digital revolution which had bound the world's economy closer together in the past two decades are going to become even more extensive and tighter. That is going to be true in the so-called service industries as well as in manufacturing.

Sol Sanders, "Globalization, Here We Come!"
World Tribune, *October 3, 2008. www.worldtribune.com.*

oped nations] simply do not reflect this changing economic architecture. Effective multilateral governance of the global economy will require institutions that do. It is 64 years since the [1944] Bretton Woods conference put in place the basic machinery of modern global economic coordination. It is time for a Bretton Woods for [the twenty-first] century.

It has always been a mistake to believe that globalisation was putting governments out of business. States and effective governance are what make globalisation possible: they preserve open markets, enforce rules and responsibilities, and manage the risks for individuals and society. We have been reminded ... that the state underpins the market as lender of last resort. But it has a legitimate claim to a wider role. Its role is to ensure that the conduct of individuals or businesses does not put at risk the stability of the system or the foundations of our economies.

What Has Been Learned

We have nothing to gain by shutting down financial globalisation. But the networks that make up globalisation will keep transmitting the shocks along with the benefits unless we take a tougher line with excessive risk, and strengthen the multilateral instruments that govern the global financial system.

If there is anything cathartic in this crisis it will be a healthy new scepticism for financial products we don't understand, a heightened intolerance for excessive risk-taking, and a new conviction that a global economy needs global economic governance.

"The policy of trade liberalization ... is warming the planet."

Globalization Is Fueling Global Warming

Les Leopold

Les Leopold is the executive director of the Labor Institute and Public Health Institute in New York and author of The Man Who Hated Work and Loved Labor: The Life and Times of Tony Mazzocchi. *In the viewpoint that follows, Leopold argues that globalized free trade may benefit multinational corporations, but it is worsening global climate change. According to Leopold, expanded trade requires more transportation fuel and entices rapidly developing nations—such as China—to build more factories and power plants to supply goods to meet global demand. Without countering the carbon dioxide emissions that result from this growth in trade, the world will suffer the negative impacts of global warming even as profits soar.*

As you read, consider the following questions:

1. How does Leopold use the shipping of high-efficiency light bulbs as an example of the folly of globalization?

Les Leopold, "Globalization Is Fueling Global Warming," AlterNet, December 28, 2007. Reproduced by permission.

2. What does the author say is wrong with the argument that global carbon "cap and trade" regulations will eventually correct the carbon emissions associated with expanding free trade?

3. According to Leopold, what should every trade agreement include?

As global warming negotiations move from Bali towards a worldwide treaty, it is important to address how global warming and global trade work hand-in-hand.

Globalization is to global warming what warm water in the Gulf of Mexico waters was to Hurricane Katrina. And, unless we wisely limit rapidly accelerating global trade, we will see equally disastrous and deadly results—worsening global warming and a continued chemical poisoning of our world.

Policy Warms the Planet

For nearly a generation, the mainstream pro-globalization forces have ignored climate change. Instead we've been bombarded with the virtues of liberalized trade: It drives down prices, increases efficiency, lifts nations out of poverty, and contributes to overall global prosperity. Those who questioned NAFTA [North American Free Trade Agreement], CAFTA [Central American Free Trade Agreement], GATT [General Agreement on Tariffs and Trade], and the like are derided as "protectionists," who force artificially high prices on the rest of us while making our economy less competitive. Manufacturing unions attempting to stop the destruction of millions of middle-income, U.S.-based factory jobs are vilified as elitists who are more concerned about the privileged few than about the poor who gain new jobs in developing nations.

The subtext of the messaging is clear: globalization is our fate, and there are no effective controls. Only a foolish Luddite [one who reacts against modernization] would stand in its way, we are told.

Missing from this narrative, as Zbigniew Brzezinski, the former national security adviser to Jimmy Carter, has pointed out, is that globalization is a policy, not an act of God. He is right. Human policy-making shapes expanding world trade. And the policy of trade liberalization, among other things, is warming the planet.

Global free trade proponents skillfully argue for comparative advantage, opening up markets, and economies of scale. They point to the communications marvels that have flattened and shrunken the world, putting us all in contact and in competition with each other for the best ideas and products.

The Costs of Consumption

Global warming, however, puts a kink in this new global utopia because it demands that we also include the costs of externalities—the carbon dioxide [CO_2] emitted from shipping and flying goods all over the globe—goods that could easily be produced much closer to the point of consumption.

It may be marvelous to text message your colleague in Bangalore, but from a CO_2 perspective, it's folly to fly fresh raspberries from Chile to California. And under current trade policies, we will import the next wave of high-efficiency light bulbs to save energy while wasting some of the gain on the carbon used to transport them here from around the globe.

But the elephant in the room [i.e., an obvious point being ignored] is hyper-development. Expanded trade indeed has contributed to the enormous economic growth rates in China (and India). As a result, China's appetite for fuel and power has grown exponentially: As *The New York Times* reported (June 11, 2006), every week to 10 days, another coal-fired power plant comes online in China large enough to serve a major U.S. city.

Pollyannaish [absurdly optimistic] analysts argue this too will pass when global carbon cap and trading schemas are put in place, and a price, in effect, is placed on carbon emissions.

China's Pollution

China's blazing economic growth, supplying cheap products to the world, has [its share of] costs. . . . Accelerated burning of coal and use of chemicals to fuel the export machine pollute not only China's air and water but the world's environment as well. A 2004 study found that the jet stream dispersed chemicals like mercury, spewed by factories in China, to locations thousands of miles away. A researcher traced a plume of dirty air from Asia to New England, where analysis of collected samples revealed the chemicals had originated in China, reported the *Wall Street Journal* in 2004.

Nayan Chanda,
Yale Global Online, June 28, 2007.

This, we are told, will lead to a burst of new technologies and efficiencies that dramatically reduce global warming gases. Perhaps. But it seems this should have been thought through as part of trade liberalization, rather than left to the indefinite future. As a result, we are trapped in a race against the accelerating forces of rapid, carbon-fueled development unleashed by our very own trade policies.

Few Winners, Many Losers

And, it's apparent who the winners are in this race as onto our store shelves and into our homes come toxic toys, toxic pharmaceuticals, toxic toothpaste, and toxic dog food—very predictable products of accelerated global trade. It is ironic to hear pundits and politicians rage against the poor regulatory and inspection protocols in "Communist" China—the virtual hub of global capitalist production.

In fact, first world multinationals, the loudest cheerleaders for unfettered free trade, are commissioning these products and shipping them here. And as many early 20th-century muckrakers [whistle-blowing journalists] would have warned, these corporations require stringent regulation. They need to be "guided" away from the age-old temptation to cut corners, or turn a blind eye when sub-contractors use forced labor or contaminated substances. Common sense would have called for those regulations to be in place before giving the green light to the transfer of production to wherever labor was least expensive and safeguards most porous.

Already, the European Union is working to get these toxic substances out of consumer products, but the United States stands increasingly alone against such standards. And we wonder why our kids are getting sick from playthings.

The Need for Regulation

Unfettered global trade will make efforts to reverse global warming and deliver safe products to our country all the more difficult. We must start with a renunciation of our fatalism and put a halt to the name calling. In fact, we should thank the labor and environmental critics of accelerated trade for alerting us to these dangers.

Next we should insist that every trade agreement should include global warming impact studies that assess the carbon footprints of accelerated trade.

And, as many have argued, rigorous safety inspections on food, pharmaceuticals, and other consumer items must be put in place before products cross our borders.

And yes, we also will need carefully constructed border adjustment taxes so that new green, carbon-reducing industries can be nourished at home. Those high efficiency light bulbs, wind generators and solar panels should not be imported from factories tied to inefficient energy sources sent from afar on ships and planes burning fossil fuels. The next wave of green products should instead be manufactured closer to where they will be used, creating homegrown, green jobs while helping to reduce global warming.

Or we can continue waiting for the invisible hand to determine our fate—a fate that will ensure global warming to go unchecked and unabated, and more children sucking toxic toys.

"Globalization has its costs, but it also has its benefits, and among those is an international trade framework that can be used to enforce emission reductions."

Globalization Could Help Ease Global Warming

Joseph E. Stiglitz

Joseph E. Stiglitz affirms in the following viewpoint that globalization is contributing to global warming, but he insists that the international cooperation promoted by free trade could be utilized to counter climate change. In Stiglitz's view, the world should encourage globalization but impose a tax on carbon emissions associated with the production of goods. The tax would prompt all nations to embrace more efficient, less polluting methods of production, thus reducing carbon emissions while still promoting the benefits of trade. Joseph E. Stiglitz is a Nobel Prize–winning professor of economics at Columbia University. He is the author of Globalization and Its Discontents *and* Making Globalization Work.

Joseph E. Stiglitz, "How Globalization Could Help Ease Global Warming," *San Francisco Chronicle*, September 17, 2006, p. E-1. Reproduced by permission of the author.

As you read, consider the following questions:

1. What nation is the world's largest polluter, as Stiglitz affirms?

2. According to the author, why are some developing nations reacting against the restrictions of the Kyoto Protocol?

3. On what would Stiglitz like to see the proceeds from a global carbon tax spent?

Around the world, [the summer of 2006] was different: Country after country experienced the hottest weeks since records have been kept. China experienced its worst storm in fifty years. Visitors flocked to an alpine village in Switzerland to see its mountain crumble—the result of the melting of a glacier. Greenland may soon again become green. Oil companies are relishing the prospect of getting at oil beneath the Arctic Ocean, as its ice cap melts more rapidly than anyone anticipated a few years ago.

The inability to solve global warming, the most serious environmental problem facing the world, is emblematic of the failures of globalization. But it is also an opportunity to use the forces of globalization for the good of the planet's health.

We have become more interdependent, and greater interdependence increases the need for acting together. But we do not have the institutional frameworks for doing this effectively and democratically.

There has been much discussion of how we can make our global economy work more smoothly, but if we do not learn how to share our planet better, economic progress will be for naught.

Emissions of a Developing Planet

We are engaged in a grand experiment: What happens if you release carbon dioxide and certain other gases into the atmosphere in larger amounts? Scientists are fairly sure of the outcome, and it is not pretty. The gases act like a greenhouse, capturing solar energy in the atmosphere, and gradually the Earth warms up. Ocean currents are altered, ocean levels rise, rainfall patterns change, storms become more intense. Glacier National Park—Montana's million-acre reserve—will be without glaciers even before the Arctic ice cap melts, now anticipated well before the end of this century.

If we had access to a thousand planets, it might make sense to use one to conduct such an experiment. If things turned out badly—as they almost surely will—we could move on to the next. But we don't have that luxury. We're stuck here on Earth.

In Kyoto, [where the United Nations adopted its convention on climate change in 1997], the world took an important first step to curtail greenhouse gas emissions. But the United States, the world's largest polluter, refuses to join in and continues to pollute more and more, while the developing countries, which soon will be contributing 50 percent or more of global emissions, haven't made firm commitments to do anything.

America's Blissful Ignorance

We need an enforcement mechanism to prevent the United States or any other country that refuses to cut back emissions from inflicting harm on the rest of the world.

It is, perhaps, predictable that it would be the United States that refuses to recognize the existence of the problem. If the United States could go its own merry way—keeping the carbon dioxide it emits over its own territory, warming up its own atmosphere, bearing whatever costs (including hurricanes) that result, that would be one thing. The United States may intend no harm to others, but the damage from global warming to which its energy and emissions-profligate lifestyle is contributing is greater than any war could inflict.

The Maldives [islands] will within 50 years be our own 21st-century Atlantis, disappearing beneath the ocean. A third of Bangladesh, too, will be submerged, and with that country's poor people crowded closer together, incomes already close to subsistence level will be further submerged.

Some American politicians complain that emissions reduction will compromise America's living standards, but America's emissions per dollar of gross domestic product are twice that of Japan. The United States not only can afford to conserve more, that actually would enhance energy security. It would be good for its environment and for its economy—although not, perhaps, for the oil companies that have prospered so much in recent years.

When Environment Trumps Commerce

Globalization has its costs, but it also has its benefits, and among those is an international trade framework that can be used to enforce emission reductions. This framework is designed to create a level playing field. If some country subsidizes its firms, there is not a level playing field, which is why (with a few exceptions) subsidies are proscribed. But not paying the full costs of production—not paying the cost of damage to the environment—is itself a subsidy, just as not paying the full costs of workers would be.

In most developed countries today, firms are paying the cost of pollution to the global environment, in the form of taxes imposed on coal, oil and gas. American firms are effectively being subsidized—and massively so.

The United States itself has been in the forefront of advocating the principle that countries that damage the global environment should face trade sanctions. It prohibited the importation of Thai shrimp that were caught in "turtle unfriendly" nets, which caused the unnecessary deaths of large numbers of these endangered species.

Global Efforts Needed

The challenges posed by climate change, environmental protection, energy conservation, terrorism and proliferation of weapons of mass destruction are far greater than the immediate threat of conflict among nations. In a multi-faceted, multi-polar world, unilateralism would work to the detriment of achieving an international solution. . . .

In a multi-faceted, multi-polar world, collective management of international affairs makes far greater sense than the hegemony of a solitary superpower. . . .

Although developed nations such as the US must shoulder greater responsibility, global solutions demand global effort. Globalization has created fresh opportunities for global development.

Fu Mengzi, China Daily, *January 23, 2009.*

Although the manner in which the United States imposed the restriction was criticized, the World Trade Organization sustained the principle that global environmental concerns trump narrow commercial interests, as well they should. But if one can justify restricting imports of shrimp in order to protect turtles, certainly one can justify restricting imports of goods produced by technologies that unnecessarily pollute the air, in order to protect our precious global atmosphere, upon which we all depend for our very well-being.

Taxing Inefficiency

There is a second problem with Kyoto: how to bring the developing countries into the fold. The Kyoto protocol is based on national emission reductions relative to each nation's level in 1990. The developing countries ask, why should the developed countries be allowed to pollute more now simply because they polluted more in the past? Developing countries contend that because the developed countries have already contributed so much, they should face larger emission reductions.

The world seems at an impasse: The United States refuses to go along unless developing countries reduce their emissions, and the developing countries see no reason they should not be allowed to pollute as much per capita as the United States. But allowing them per capita emission levels comparable to that of the U.S. would imply that no restraints would be imposed on them for decades.

There is a way out, and that is through a common (global) environmental tax on emissions.

There is a social cost to emissions, and the common environmental tax would simply make everyone pay the social cost. This is in accord with the most basic of economic principles, that individuals and firms should pay their full costs.

The tax could be set so that the level of reductions is the same as the Kyoto targets. It would be good if the world could agree to use the proceeds to finance the range of global public goods that are so important for making globalization work better—for instance, for promoting health, research and development. But that may be too ambitious.

Alternatively, each country could keep its own revenues and use them to reduce existing taxes. It makes much more sense to tax "bads" (pollution, like greenhouse gas emissions) than to tax "goods," like work and saving. Overall economic efficiency would be increased.

The big advantage of this proposal over the Kyoto approach is that it avoids most of the debate about how much each country needs to reduce its emissions. Under Kyoto, getting the right to pollute more is, in effect, receiving an enormous gift. Now that pollution rights are tradeable, we can even put a market value on them, and it is enormous. Each country claims special circumstances that warrant a larger allocation of emission rights. But under the common tax approach, these debates are sidestepped. All that is asked is that everyone pay the social cost of their emissions.

Remaking Globalization

The challenges the world confronts in coping with global warming parallel those in the other arenas of globalization: an unfair global trade regime that impedes development, an unstable global financial system that results in crisis after crisis, with poor countries repeatedly finding themselves with debt burdens beyond their ability to pay, and a global intellectual property regime which denies access to affordable lifesaving drugs, even as the AIDS epidemic ravages so much of the developing world.

We have seen the anomalies. Money should flow from the rich to the poor countries, but in recent years, it has been going in the opposite direction. Because the rich are better able to bear the risk of exchange and interest rate fluctuations, the rich should bear the brunt of this volatility, but instead it is borne by the poor. Resource rich countries have done more poorly than those who are far worse off.

Globalization can be changed; indeed, it is clear that it will be changed. The question is: Will change be forced upon us, a result of a crisis, or will we take control of the process? The former risks a backlash against globalization or a haphazard reshaping, in a way that only sets the stage for even more problems in the future. The latter holds out the possibility of remaking globalization so that it at last lives up to its potential of improving the living standards of everyone in the world—and as an added benefit helping to save the atmosphere that makes life on Earth possible.

"*Globalization . . . is fully to blame both for terrorism and for the war against it.*"

Globalization Promotes Terrorism

Kevin Potvin

In the following viewpoint, Kevin Potvin contends that globalization is exacerbating the sense of cultural alienation and social dissociation felt by many of the world's people. Potvin claims that rampant consumerism reinforces alienation by providing products—everything from drugs to televisions—that cater to a sense of isolation or not-belonging. In Potvin's view, fanatics— especially in less consumerist societies—eventually react against globalization's dissociation and employ terrorism to strike back at this money-centered ideology. Kevin Potvin is the editor of the Republic of East Vancouver, *a Canadian print and online newspaper.*

As you read, consider the following questions:

1. Why does Potvin believe it is wrong to single out Islamism as inherently opposed to globalization?

Kevin Potvin, "Globalization and Its Promoters Have Bred Terrorism," *Republic of East Vancouver*, vol. 143, July 20–August 2, 2006. Reproduced by permission.

2. According to the author, what are some examples of growing cultural embeddedness and social connectivity that are absent in globalized communities today?

3. How does Potvin use the thought of Émile Durkheim to help target globalization as a chief cause of terrorism in the modern world?

There was always one complaint protesters made against globalization, lo those many years ago, that promoters of globalization never answered: the homogenizing effect of globalization would bring heightened cultural alienation and rising social dissociation everywhere. Yes, they also complained it would make some people or nations poorer, a complaint globalization's promoters focused exclusively on and easily defeated, for it is true that increased trade generally increases prosperity. But the first charge should have been paid more attention to.

Alienation Breeds Fanaticism

The once-rollicking anti-globalization movement was vaporized in the blasts of 9/11, but its predictions have nonetheless come harrowingly true. Mistaken as virulent Islamism, or more generally as religious fanaticism, riots in the suburbs of Paris and on the beaches of Sydney, as well as bombs on the trains of London and bomb plots hatched in Toronto, no less than American Jews moving to occupation settlements in Palestine and "Support our Troops" t-shirts being sold in Parksville, BC [British Columbia], are very much about cultural alienation and social dissociation brought on by globalization, and are only incidentally about Islam and hate-preaching Imams [Muslim clerics].

The Muslim cloak enshrouding the latest events could have been any religious cloak in any other era, for all religions lend themselves to violent subversion of secular power when the need arises, even Christianity, even Buddhism. Religious fervor rises up wherever social and cultural glues dissolve. By focusing on questions of whether Islam does or does not condone violence for this or that situation, the public, their pundits, and even prime ministers (including [Canada's]) miss the forest for the trees. The rise of religious fanaticism anywhere, including in the American south as much as in the Middle East, is evidence of high cultural alienation and spreading social dissociation.

A Key Function of Capitalism

Promoters of globalization would not answer to the charge that globalization will dissolve social and cultural glues because that is an acknowledged key function of capitalism itself. A vast proportion of retail sales of consumer products—the engine of capitalism—result from, and serve to assuage feelings of, alienation and dissociation throughout all economic classes, the rich no less than the poor. Because they serve the needs of the capitalist economic system so well, behaviors and conditions that promote alienation and dissociation are encouraged (even if unwittingly) by political and other leaders. Or at the very least, behaviors and conditions that promote social integration and create cultural embeddedness are neglected, defunded, and left to atrophy, since they serve no immediately measurable economic good in a classic capitalist society.

Cars promoted as objects of self-expression, even to the point of vulgarity, as in the Hummer, shopping encouraged as an act of leisure itself, and the marketing of drugs to combat every conceivable negative thought, are examples of a society in which alienation and dissociation are being encouraged. On the contrary, high voter turnouts at all levels of elections, robust and evolving community centres, and expanding public systems like transit, health and education, are signs of a society in which cultural embeddedness and social connections are growing. But along with the growth of social and cultural

Globalization and Terror

Globalization is coupled with an ideology of free markets and free trade and a decline in state intervention. According to globalization advocates, reducing international regulations and barriers to trade and investment will increase trade and development. But these very conditions that promote a globalized environment are crucial to the expansion of crime. Crime groups and terrorists have exploited the enormous decline in regulations, the lessened border controls, and the resultant greater freedom, to expand their activities across borders and to new regions of the world. These contacts have become more frequent, and the speed at which they occur has accelerated. Whereas the growth of legal trade is regulated by adherence to border control policies, customs officials, and bureaucratic systems, transnational crime groups freely exploit the loopholes of state-based legal systems to extend their reach. They travel to regions where they cannot be extradited, base their operations in countries with ineffective or corrupt law enforcement, and launder their money in countries with bank secrecy or few effective controls. By segmenting their operations, both criminals and terrorists reap the benefits of globalization, while simultaneously reducing their operational risks.

Louise Shelley,
eJournal USA, *February 2006.*

standards comes a decline in sales of goods that serve as substitutes when those standards are in decline, like Hummers, televisions, drugs and iPods—and classic capitalism cannot be sustained in a milieu of declining consumer demand.

Social and Cultural Decline

Social connectivity and cultural embeddedness are not nearly as easy to measure as economic growth, nor do we have as vocal and powerful a cadre of spokespeople clamoring about them as we do spokespeople shouting about economic growth. Nor are we nearly as aware of the deleterious effects of declining social and cultural standards as we are of the effects of declining economic standards. We know each week if we are able to buy as much, and by exactly how much we are short. But it usually takes years for the effects of declining social and cultural standards to be noticed, and then only in indirect and indeterminate ways. Minute movements in stockmarkets and currencies around the world are reported every fifteen minutes on radio stations in every city, but never are movements in social capital or cultural currency reported.

But those effects are surely noticeable when they do arrive. Riots in Paris and Sydney, bombs in Bali and London, and plots hatched in Toronto, no less than bunker busters dropped on Afghan and Iraqi neighbourhoods and prisoners captured by Canadian troops and handed over to American torture chambers, are the visible signs of a generation-long decline in cultural and social standards of living (even while economic standards of living could well be rising in every one of these places). They are the manifestation of results of globalization as predicted by anti-globalization activists for two decades prior to 9/11. Described variously by authorities in Canada and abroad as terrorism (homegrown or foreign), Islamism, religious fanaticism, hatred and medievalism, these events are none of these as much as they are the flipside of thoroughly modern globalization. And that which passes as terrorism is a thoroughly modern reply. Émile Durkheim, in his seminal 1905 book *Suicide*, which every university undergraduate in the last three decades has surely read, made the point that while we might find the cause of each individual suicide in the minute details of a life, to understand why different societies had different overall rates of suicide, an accumulation of those individual details told us nothing. We needed, he wrote, to identify causes on the national level to understand national-level effects. And so it is with so-called terrorism. We can bicker about the individual causes of this or that particular person who decides to take up violence against economic and state symbols, but the accumulation of such individual causes will tell us nothing about why the effects are spreading globally. To understand the phenomenon of "terrorism" on its global level, we need to identify a global cause to explain it. And that cause is none other than that set of policies falling under the rubric of economic globalization as promoted and pushed around the world beginning two decades ago, in 1986, with the signing of the first NAFTA [North American Free Trade Agreement] agreement.

Warnings Signs There

All the unthinking promoters of globalization, and all their dollar-sign-blinded defenders in the media over the last two decades—all those newspaper columnists and radio show hosts, the learned authors of journal articles, the speechmakers, the analysts and the economists, the professors and their graduate students, and all the think tanks, media companies, and universities, as well as all the companies that underwrote them with bursaries and grants—are directly to blame for the rising death toll and the spreading culture of fear due to the twin phenomena of terrorism and war at home and abroad.

Critics of globalization warned repeatedly and convincingly that globalization would send into a hyperdriven offensive the already deleterious effects of capitalism on social and cultural standards, effects that would come to be felt in ways that would make the economic gains of globalization pale in comparison. Those critics were routinely abused in the media, ignored in the universities, and dismissed in the think tanks, and their warnings were never answered. Just as [George W.

Bush's secretary of state] Condoleezza Rice could say with a straight face that nobody in her administration had conceived that anyone would ever fly a plane into a building as an act of terrorism, so too might promoters of globalization claim that they never conceived of homegrown terrorism, bombings, or threats of prime ministerial beheadings as the direct results of globalization. But on both claims we know they were fully warned.

What the alarmed leaders today call terrorism is nothing more, nor less, than the next stage of protest against globalization. And what we are today alarmed to see perpetrated in the name of anti-terrorism—the destruction of civil rights, the transformation of our economies into war economies, the forced deposing of foreign governments, the waging of brutal war around the world, and the outright mass murder of innocent civilians—is only the next stage in the globalization agenda. None of this has anything to do with religion, freedom, hatred, or economic well-being or the lack of it. It is all about economic globalization and the negative effects of it on our social and cultural standards of living, and the reaction against these, only with the intensity on both sides ratcheted up a few levels since the Battle in Seattle of 1999 [where massive protests disturbed a world trade summit].

Hunting Down the Blameworthy

Globalization's critics were silenced in the blasts of 9/11, but perhaps its time to stand them up and dust them off again to hear what they have to say, seeing as how they were right. An end to the violence perpetrated, and in turn encouraged, by globalization's promoters the last two decades will only come when globalization's promoters are finally rejected, ridiculed, and marginalized right out of the media, the universities, and the halls of government power. Globalization is a monumental failure that has brought us to this point of massive violence, death and fear around the world. All its promoters the last two decades should be hunted down and held up against the wall to answer for these awful crimes. It is not the religious Islamists we need to smoke out, but the economic globalists, and it is the globalists' ideology that needs to be repudiated, not the ideology of those who are only replying to globalization's offensive. It is everyone who has promoted globalization the last twenty years who is fully to blame both for terrorism and for the war against it.

"A shift in the global balance of power would . . . help the United States manage . . . the most costly and dangerous consequences of globalization."

America Cannot Manage Globalization Alone

Steven Weber, Naazneen Barma, Matthew Kroenig, and Ely Ratner

Steven Weber is a professor of political science and director of the Institute for International Studies at the University of California, Berkeley. Naazneen Barma, Matthew Kroenig, and Ely Ratner are PhD candidates at Berkeley and research fellows at the university's New Era Foreign Policy Center. *In the viewpoint that follows, Weber and his colleagues contend that in a globalized world, the United States' position as the last superpower is a hindrance, not a help, to foreign policy. The authors argue that America does not have the power to monitor all the problems that globalization creates, nor does it have the influence to secure the goodwill of all other nations so that global problems can be redressed. Weber and his coauthors go so far as to claim that America's superpower status encourages other nations to find ways to curb U.S. power. According to the authors, only an in-*

Steven Weber et al., "How Globalization Went Bad," *Foreign Policy*, vol. 158, January/ February 2007, pp. 48–54. Copyright © 2008 Foreign Policy. All rights reserved. Reproduced by permission.

ternational balance of power—perhaps through the rise of another superpower—will ease globalization and remove the burden of its failures from U.S. shoulders alone.

As you read, consider the following questions:

1. What do Weber and his colleagues mean when they write, "A world of several great powers is a more interest-rich environment"?

2. Why do the authors state that North Korea did not seek nuclear weapons during the Cold War but are seeking them now?

3. In the authors' opinion, why does the terrorist group al Qaeda see the United States as the "only enemy worth fighting"?

The world today is more dangerous and less orderly than it was supposed to be. [In the early-to-mid 1990s], the naive expectations were that the "end of history" was near. The reality has been the opposite. The world has more international terrorism and more nuclear proliferation today than it did in 1990. International institutions are weaker. The threats of pandemic disease and climate change are stronger. Cleavages of religious and cultural ideology are more intense. The global financial system is more unbalanced and precarious.

It wasn't supposed to be like this. The end of the Cold War was supposed to make global politics and economics easier to manage, not harder. What went wrong? The bad news of the 21st century is that globalization has a significant dark side. The container ships that carry manufactured Chinese goods to and from the United States also carry drugs. The airplanes that fly passengers nonstop from New York to Singapore also transport infectious diseases. And the Internet has proved just as adept at spreading deadly, extremist ideologies as it has e-commerce.

America's Globalized World

The conventional belief is that the single greatest challenge of geopolitics today is managing this dark side of globalization, chipping away at the illegitimate co-travelers that exploit openness, mobility, and freedom, without putting too much sand in the gears. The current U.S. strategy is to push for more trade, more connectivity, more markets, and more openness. America does so for a good reason—it benefits from globalization more than any other country in the world. The United States acknowledges globalization's dark side but attributes it merely to exploitation behavior by criminals, religious extremists, and other anachronistic elements that can be eliminated. The dark side of globalization, America says, with very little subtlety, can be mitigated by the expansion of American power, sometimes unilaterally and sometimes through multilateral institutions, depending on how the United States likes it. In other words, America is aiming for a "flat," globalized world coordinated by a single superpower.

That's nice work if you can get it. But the United States almost certainly cannot. Not only because other countries won't let it, but, more profoundly, because that line of thinking is faulty. The predominance of American power has many benefits, but the management of globalization is not one of them. The mobility of ideas, capital, technology, and people is hardly new. But the rapid advance of globalization's evils is. Most of that advance has taken place since 1990. Why? Because what changed profoundly in the 1990s was the polarity of the international system. For the first time in modern history, globalization was superimposed onto a world with a single superpower. What we have discovered [since the early 1990s] is that it is a dangerous mixture. The negative effects of globalization since 1990 are not the result of globalization itself. They are the dark side of American predominance.

The Dangers of Unipolarity

A straightforward piece of logic from market economics helps explain why unipolarity and globalization don't mix. Monopolies, regardless of who holds them, are almost always bad for both the market and the monopolist. We propose three simple axioms of "globalization under unipolarity" that reveal these dangers.

Axiom 1: Above a certain threshold of power, the rate at which new global problems are generated will exceed the rate at which old problems are fixed. Power does two things in international politics: It enhances the capability of a state to do things, but it also increases the number of things that a state must worry about. At a certain point, the latter starts to overtake the former. It's the familiar law of diminishing returns. Because powerful states have large spheres of influence and their security and economic interests touch every region of the world, they are threatened by the risk of things going wrong—anywhere. That is particularly true for the United States, which leverages its ability to go anywhere and do anything through massive debt. No one knows exactly when the law of diminishing returns will kick in. But, historically, it starts to happen long before a single great power dominates the entire globe, which is why large empires from Byzantium to Rome have always reached a point of unsustainability.

That may already be happening to the United States today, on issues ranging from oil dependency and nuclear proliferation to pandemics and global warming. What Axiom 1 tells you is that more U.S. power is not the answer; it's actually part of the problem. A multipolar world would almost certainly manage the globe's pressing problems more effectively. The larger the number of great powers in the global system, the greater the chance that at least one of them would exercise some control over a given combination of space, other actors, and problems. Such reasoning doesn't rest on hopeful notions that the great powers will work together. They might do so. But even if they don't, the result is distributed governance, where some great power is interested in most every part of the world through productive competition.

Axiom 2: In an increasingly networked world, places that fall between the networks are very dangerous places—and there will be more ungoverned zones when there is only one network to join. The second axiom acknowledges that highly connected networks can be efficient, robust, and resilient to shocks. But in a highly connected world, the pieces that fall between the networks are increasingly shut off from the benefits of connectivity. These problems fester in the form of failed states, mutate like pathogenic bacteria, and, in some cases, reconnect in subterranean networks such as [the terrorist group] al Qaeda. The truly dangerous places are the points where the subterranean networks touch the mainstream of global politics and economics. What made Afghanistan so dangerous under the Taliban was not that it was a failed state. It wasn't. It was a partially failed and partially connected state that worked the interstices of globalization through the drug trade, counterfeiting, and terrorism.

Can any single superpower monitor all the seams and back alleys of globalization? Hardly. In fact, a lone hegemon is unlikely to look closely at these problems, because more pressing issues are happening elsewhere, in places where trade and technology are growing. By contrast, a world of several great powers is a more interest-rich environment in which nations must look in less obvious places to find new sources of advantage. In such a system, it's harder for troublemakers to spring up, because the cracks and seams of globalization are held together by stronger ties.

Axiom 3: Without a real chance to find useful allies to counter a superpower, opponents will try to neutralize power, by going underground, going nuclear, or going "bad." Axiom 3 is a story about the preferred strategies of the weak. It's a basic insight of international relations that states try to balance power. They protect themselves by joining groups that can hold a hegemonic threat at bay. But what if there is no viable group to join? In today's unipolar world, every nation from Venezuela to North Korea is looking for a way to constrain American power. But in the unipolar world, it's harder for states to join together to do that. So they turn to other means. They play a different game. Hamas [the militant rulers of the Palestinian territories], Iran, Somalia, North Korea, and Venezuela are not going to become allies anytime soon. Each is better off finding other ways to make life more difficult for Washington. Going nuclear is one way. Counterfeiting U.S. currency is another. Raising uncertainty about oil supplies is perhaps the most obvious method of all.

Here's the important downside of unipolar globalization. In a world with multiple great powers, many of these threats would be less troublesome. The relatively weak states would have a choice among potential partners with which to ally, enhancing their influence. Without that more attractive choice, facilitating the dark side of globalization becomes the most effective means of constraining American power.

Sharing the Burden

The world is paying a heavy price for the instability created by the combination of globalization and unipolarity, and the United States is bearing most of the burden. Consider the case of nuclear proliferation. There's effectively a market out there for proliferation, with its own supply (states willing to share nuclear technology) and demand (states that badly want a nuclear weapon). The overlap of unipolarity with globalization ratchets up both the supply and demand, to the detriment of U.S. national security.

It has become fashionable, in the wake of the Iraq war, to comment on the limits of conventional military force. But much of this analysis is overblown. The United States may not be able to stabilize and rebuild Iraq. But that doesn't matter much from the perspective of a government that thinks the Pentagon has it in its sights. In Tehran [Iran], Pyongyang [North Korea], and many other capitals, including Beijing, the bottom line is simple: The U.S. military could, with conventional force, end those regimes tomorrow if it chose to do so. No country in the world can dream of challenging U.S. conventional military power. But they can certainly hope to deter America from using it. And the best deterrent yet invented is the threat of nuclear retaliation. Before 1989, states that felt threatened by the United States could turn to the Soviet Union's nuclear umbrella for protection. Now, they turn to people like A.Q. Khan [Pakistani scientist who reportedly sold nuclear secrets to Iran, North Korea, and other nations]. Having your own nuclear weapon used to be a luxury. Today, it is fast becoming a necessity.

North Korea is the clearest example. Few countries had it worse during the Cold War. North Korea was surrounded by feuding, nuclear-armed communist neighbors, it was officially at war with its southern neighbor, and it stared continuously at tens of thousands of U.S. troops on its border. But, for 40 years, North Korea didn't seek nuclear weapons. It didn't need to, because it had the Soviet nuclear umbrella. Within five years of the Soviet collapse, however; Pyongyang was pushing ahead full steam on plutonium reprocessing facilities. North Korea's founder, Kim Il Sung, barely flinched when former U.S. President Bill Clinton's administration readied war plans to strike his nuclear installations preemptively. That brinkmanship paid off. Today North Korea is likely a nuclear power, and Kim's son rules the country with an iron fist. America's conventional military strength means a lot less to a nuclear North Korea. [Iraq's former dictator] Saddam Hussein's great strategic blunder was that he took too long to get to the same place.

Dividing Up the Burden

How would things be different in a multipolar world? For starters, great powers could split the job of policing proliferation, and even collaborate on some particularly hard cases. It's often forgotten now that, during the Cold War, the only state with a tougher nonproliferation policy than the United States was the Soviet Union. Not a single country that had a formal alliance with Moscow ever became a nuclear power. The Eastern bloc was full of countries with advanced technological capabilities in every area except one—nuclear weapons. Moscow simply wouldn't permit it. But today we see the uneven and inadequate level of effort that non-superpowers devote to stopping proliferation. The Europeans dangle carrots at Iran, but they are unwilling to consider serious sticks. The Chinese refuse to admit that there is a problem. And the Russians are aiding Iran's nuclear ambitions. When push comes to shove, nonproliferation today is almost entirely America's burden.

Diseases America Cannot Control

The same is true for global public health. Globalization is turning the world into an enormous petri dish for the incubation of infectious disease. Humans cannot outsmart disease, because it just evolves too quickly. Bacteria can reproduce a new generation in less than 30 minutes, while it takes us decades to come up with a new generation of antibiotics. Solutions are only possible when and where we get the upper hand. Poor countries where humans live in close proximity to farm animals are the best place to breed extremely dangerous zoonotic [animal-originated] disease. These are often the same countries, perhaps not entirely coincidentally, that feel threatened by American power. Establishing an early warning system for these diseases—exactly what we lacked in the case of SARS [severe acute respiratory syndrome outbreak in 2002–2003] and exactly what we lack for avian flu today—will require a significant level of intervention into the very places

Globalization

that don't want it. That will be true as long as international intervention means American interference.

The most likely sources of the next ebola or HIV-like pandemic are the countries that simply won't let U.S. or other Western agencies in, including the World Health Organization. Yet the threat is too arcane and not immediate enough for the West to force the issue. What's needed is another great power to take over a piece of the work, a power that has more immediate interests in the countries where diseases incubate and one that is seen as less of a threat. As long as the United States remains the world's lone superpower, we're not likely to get any help. Even after HIV, SARS, and several years of mounting hysteria about avian flu, the world is still not ready for a viral pandemic in Southeast Asia or sub-Saharan Africa. America can't change that alone.

Violent Reactions to American Power

If there were rival great powers with different cultural and ideological leanings, globalization's darkest problem of all—terrorism—would also likely look quite different. The pundits are partly right: Today's international terrorism owes something to globalization. Al Qaeda uses the Internet to transmit messages, it uses credit cards and modern banking to move money, and it uses cell phones and laptops to plot attacks. But it's not globalization that turned [al Qaeda leader] Osama bin Laden from a small-time Saudi dissident into the symbolic head of a radical global movement. What created Osama bin Laden was the predominance of American power.

A terrorist organization needs a story to attract resources and recruits. Oftentimes, mere frustration over political, economic, or religious conditions is not enough. Al Qaeda understands that, and, for that reason, it weaves a narrative of global jihad against a "modernization," "Westernization," and a "Judeo-Christian" threat. There is really just one country that both spearheads and represents that threat: the United States.

The Need to Narrow the Gap Between Rich and Poor

While the US cannot maintain its hegemonic status forever and states will continue to shift between the core and semi-periphery, a more equal distribution of wealth will not occur on its own. In the current age of advanced technologies where images of American wealth are beamed across the globe, conflict is a natural outcome of such dramatic inequalities. . . . Today, globalization is being challenged around the world. Meetings of the institutions of globalization—the World Bank and the IMF [International Monetary Fund]—are met with intense violence and outrage. Those who see globalization as a force that has brought poverty to large parts of the world will continue to oppose it unless something is done to narrow the gap between the rich and the poor. If ideology continues to take precedence over pragmatism, conflict is an inevitable outcome. Just as other market-dominant minorities in history [have done], the United States and other core states will always provoke intense resentments. The age of terrorism has brought with it the possibility that richer countries will be awakened to the plight of those countries that live in the periphery observing the displays wealth exhibited by the rich nations operating in the core of the world system. No longer is narrowing the gap between rich and poor countries merely the humane and benevolent thing to do, it has become a matter of self-preservation for the rich countries.

Arthur L. Dunklin, "Globalization: A Portrait of Exploitation, Inequality, and Limits," Globalization, Fall 2005.

And so the most efficient way for a terrorist to gain a reputation is to attack the United States. The logic is the same for all monopolies. A few years ago, every computer hacker in the world wanted to bring down Microsoft, just as every aspiring terrorist wants to create a spectacle of destruction akin to the September 11 attacks inside the United States.

Al Qaeda cells have gone after alternate targets such as Britain, Egypt, and Spain. But these are not the acts that increase recruitment and fundraising, or mobilize the energy of otherwise disparate groups around the world. Nothing enhances the profile of a terrorist like killing an American, something Abu Musab al-Zarqawi [an Islamic militant leader known for carrying out bombings and beheadings] understood well in Iraq. Even if al Qaeda's deepest aspirations lie with the demise of the Saudi regime, the predominance of U.S. power and its role supporting the house of Saud makes America the only enemy really worth fighting. A multipolar world would surely confuse this kind of clear framing that pits Islamism against the West. What would be al Qaeda's message if the Chinese were equally involved in propping up authoritarian regimes in the Islamic, oil-rich Gulf states? Does the al Qaeda story work if half its enemy is neither Western nor Christian?

Restoring the Balance

The consensus today in the U.S. foreign-policy community is that more American power is always better. Across the board. For both the United States and the rest of the globe. The National Security Strategy documents of 2002 and 2006 enshrine this consensus in phrases such as "a balance of power that favors freedom." The strategy explicitly defines the "balance" as a continued imbalance, as the United States continues "dissuading potential competitors . . . from challenging the United States, its allies, and its partners."

In no way is U.S. power inherently a bad thing. Nor is it true that no good comes from unipolarity. But there are significant downsides to the imbalance of power. That view is hardly revolutionary. It has a long pedigree in U.S. foreign-policy thought. It was the perspective, for instance, that George Kennan [a U.S. diplomat famed for his "containment" theory for restricting Communist expansion] brought to the table in the late 1940s when he talked about the desirability of a European superpower to restrain the United States. Although the issues today are different than they were in Kennan's time, it's still the case that too much power may, as Kennan believed, lead to overreach. It may lead to arrogance. It may lead to insensitivity to the concerns of others. Though Kennan may have been prescient to voice these concerns, he couldn't have predicted the degree to which American unipolarity would lead to such an unstable overlap with modern-day globalization.

America has experienced this dangerous burden [since the early 1990s], but it still refuses to see it for what it really is. Antiglobalization sentiment is coming today from both the right and the left. But by blaming globalization for what ails the world, the U.S. foreign-policy community is missing a very big part of what is undermining one of the most hopeful trends in modern history—the reconnection of societies, economies, and minds that political borders have kept apart for far too long.

America cannot indefinitely stave off the rise of another superpower. But, in today's networked and interdependent world, such an event is not entirely a cause for mourning. A shift in the global balance of power would, in fact, help the United States manage some of the most costly and dangerous consequences of globalization. As the international playing field levels, the scope of these problems and the threat they pose to America will only decrease. When that happens, the United States will find globalization is a far easier burden to bear.

Periodical Bibliography

The following articles have been selected to supplement the diverse views presented in this chapter.

Gordon Brown   "Managing the Birth Pangs of the New Global Order," *NPQ: New Perspectives Quarterly*, Winter 2009.

Pablo Gutman   "Trade Liberalisation, Rural Poverty, and the Environment: Global Discussions and Local Cases," *Development in Practice*, November 2008.

Edward Hadas   "Life After the Meltdown," *Fortune*, January 19, 2009.

Anil Hira   "Dislocations and the Global Economy," *Futurist*, May/June 2007.

Charles S. Maier   "Dark Power," *Harvard International Review*, Spring 2007.

Floyd Norris   "The Upside to Resisting Globalization," *New York Times*, February 6, 2009.

Andrew Simms   "Global Warming: Make the Guilty Pay," *New Statesman*, December 8, 2003.

Gar Smith   "Globalization's Carbon Bootprint," *Earth Island Journal*, Summer 2008.

Katherine F. Smith   "Globalization of Human Infectious Disease," *Ecology*, August 2007.

Richard D. Smith,   "Trade and Health: An Agenda for Action,"
Kelley Lee, and Nick   *Lancet*, February 28, 2009.
Drager

Alan Sorensen   "A Panic Made in America," *Current History*, January 2009.

**OPPOSING
VIEWPOINTS®
SERIES**

CHAPTER 3

How Does Globalization Affect Developing Nations?

Chapter Preface

Under Communist leader Mao Zedong, China was a relatively closed nation. During the decade of Mao's Cultural Revolution (1966–1976), China's middle class was eradicated, and the huge peasant class was driven into specialized communes to boost agricultural and industrial production for the homeland. But what was meant to be a "Great Leap Forward" turned out to be an economic disaster. Forcing often untrained millions into state-controlled farming and steel production and giving them no way to rise above their toil left the populace disenchanted. Coupled with purges of intellectuals, the disruption of education, and bureaucratic graft and mismanagement, the lack of incentive stagnated China's economic growth potential.

In 1978—two years after Mao's death—China's new leader, Deng Xiaoping, tried to relieve China's suffering by doing away with a planned economy and opening up the nation to global markets. Deng's "Open Door Policy" reestablished cross-border trade and allowed even private firms in China to deal in goods with foreign countries. The new policy also encouraged foreign investment in Chinese companies. For more than two decades, China's imports and exports grew at astounding rates. In 1978 China's foreign trade totaled just over $20 billion; by 2001 the figure was nearly $509 billion. And in that year China was admitted into the World Trade Organization, a move that Mao would have disdained.

China's embrace of globalization has transformed the country. William H. Overholt, Rand Corporation's director of Asia Pacific Policy has stated, "Never in world history have so many workers improved their standards of living so rapidly." With the communal system destroyed, private businesses have flourished and a thriving middle class has again arisen. And this middle class—exposed to foreign goods—has a desire to keep trade open. Along with the importation of foreign products has come a cultural exchange. As Overholt claims, "The exposure of the Chinese population to foreign brands has been incorporating them into global culture." China's once-insular society is becoming part of a global society.

During this period of rapid transition, Chinese leaders have not abandoned their socialist leanings. Although the economy has changed from Mao's blueprint, party rhetoric still demands that the new era of globalization be suited to the ideal of advancing all workers. At a Chinese economic conference in 2003, Zha Peixin, the ambassador to the United Kingdom, remarked how changes in economic regulation should serve the national plan. He claimed, "The reason why China can achieve so much in such a short span of time and in a constantly changing international environment is because China has found its own road of development, suitable to its national conditions, namely building socialism with Chinese characteristics." He advocated that the reforms necessary to maintain a globalized economy would be geared "to achieve [the] self-perfection of socialism."

China's progress as a developing nation is somewhat unique. Only India has experienced a similar explosion of growth due to globalization. Most developing countries in Asia and Africa have not witnessed such profound changes, though they have struggled to balance the benefits and drawbacks of sweeping economic reform. In the following chapter, promoters and critics of globalization debate the impact such reforms are having in nations that have opened their markets to the world.

"*Free trade enables capital to come to those who need it most.*"

Globalization Benefits Developing Nations

Steven Horwitz

Steven Horwitz is a professor of economics at St. Lawrence University in Canton, New York. In the following viewpoint, he states that living conditions worldwide have improved because of globalization. Conceding that international free trade has benefited some actors more than others, Horwitz blames formal trade regulations for denying Third World nations certain advantages that he believes naturally accompany free trade, including more jobs, cheaper goods, better pay, and environmental and political security. Although multinational corporations profit from the cheap labor available in less developed countries, the author claims, it is also in their interest to invest in the workers' communities.

As you read, consider the following questions:

1. What is "comparative advantage," as Horwitz defines it?

Steven Horwitz, "Free Trade and the Climb out of Poverty," *The Freeman*, March 2005.

2. Why, in the author's view, are claims that free trade maximizes profits at human expense irrelevant?

3. How does free trade undermine the incentives of warfare, according to Horwitz?

Over the thousands of years of human history, poverty and early death have been the norm, with comfort and longevity the exceptions. The improvements in the human condition, at least on average, seen over the course of the twentieth century dwarf the improvements of the previous centuries combined. By virtually any measure one can imagine, human beings are living longer, better lives than at any other time. However, the wonders of the last century certainly did not touch all humanity equally. The clear majority of the world's population, though better off than 100 years earlier, still have lives a far cry from those of even the poorest in the West and North. One of the most pressing questions of this century is how we can extend the bounty of last century to those who have not yet been able to enjoy fully the fruits of human improvement.

At center stage in the debate over this issue is the role of "free trade" in generating or retarding human improvement. The concern, and protests in the streets, over "globalization" reflect the perceived centrality of international economic activity in understanding what makes people better off. As trade across national borders continues to grow, there are those who see in that growth the attempt by Western corporations and quasigovernmental institutions such as the International Monetary Fund (IMF) and World Bank to extract resources from the rest of the world for their own use, leaving those who already have a long hill to climb even farther from the top.

In addition, recent "free trade" agreements like NAFTA [North American Free Trade Agreement] and the proposed FTAA (Free Trade Area of the Americas) complicate matters even more by simultaneously opening up trade and heavily regulating the trade now opened. Critics of free trade and so-called "profit-led" globalization are sometimes correct in pointing to the harmful effects of the IMF and World Bank, and the clear corporate special interests that are embodied in particular agreements. However, when those criticisms are extended to genuine free trade rightly understood, they miss the mark. Attempts to restrict such trade, or to "direct it from below," are bound to worsen the condition of those people who can afford it least. Although free trade is not sufficient to ensure economic and social well-being, it is a necessary means to that end.

The Upside of Low Wages

The key to free trade's liberating role is that those who possess capital are able to bring it to workers who lack it, which in turn raises their productivity and enhances their earning power. Underlying the argument for free trade is the principle of comparative advantage, which argues that all parties are better off when each producer does what he or she does *comparatively* best and trades the results with others. Specialization by comparative advantage enables each person, or state/province, or country to find what they do at least cost and to benefit from the ability to exchange for what others can produce cheaply. . . .

For many Third World countries, their comparative advantage is the cheapness of their labor and the availability of some natural resources. For Western firms, this presents an opportunity for profit by reducing labor and resource costs. When Western firms open up shop in the Third World, they bring capital to those places. This creates jobs for citizens there and provides the West with cheaper goods. It is the classic mutual benefit of all exchange: the developing country gets jobs; the home country gets cheaper goods. The jobs created by Western firms in low-income countries average about eight

The Capitalist Peace Theory

Trade or economic interdependence plays a pivotal role in the prevention of war, because it exerts direct *and* indirect pacifying effects. In addition to the direct effect, there is the indirect effect of free trade on smaller risks of military conflict mediated by growth, prosperity, and democracy. Since the exploitation of gains from trade is the essence or purpose of capitalism and free markets, I label the sum of the direct and indirect international security benefits "the capitalist peace," of which "the democratic peace" [theory that democracies are unlikely to war against each other] merely is a component. Even if the direct 'peace by trade'-effect *were* eliminated by future research, economic freedom and globalization would still retain their crucial role in overcoming mass poverty and establishing the prerequisites of the democratic peace.

Erich Weede, Friedrich Naumann Foundation, 2005.

times the per capita wages of the local area, providing a significant benefit to those who take such jobs in comparison to their other options. . . .

Unexpected Benefits

Free trade enables capital to come to those who need it most. In addition, the very profits that Western firms make in developing countries can be a long-run source of growth for those countries. Firms that operate there frequently "recycle" their profits back into investment in better technology and equipment in those countries. It is often cheaper for the firms to invest their own profits than to use formal banking institutions because the rate of indigenous savings is low and the financial institutional structure is often weak or nonexistent.

Despite the claim of anti-globalization forces that free trade "puts profit before people," there is not a choice between "profits" and "people." Profits legitimately made in the market are a symbol of having created value and served people, and those same profits can be used in the future to make others better off. None of this assumes that Western firms are angelic, only self-interested. What the critics of globalization fail to recognize is that markets generate beneficial results as *unintended* consequences of the self-interested behavior of firms and individuals. . . .

The overwhelming empirical evidence of what is called the Environmental Kuznets Curve [shows one such unintended benefit]. In country after country we see a U-shaped relationship between per capita income and environmental quality. As growth takes place, measures of environmental quality fall, but at about $5,000 per capita GDP [gross domestic product] this turns around, with almost all categories of environmental damage showing improvement at about $8,000. Although there will be short-run costs, in the long run the path to environmental protection is paved with economic growth. Free trade promotes that growth and thus will create the wealth necessary for clean technologies. To burden the developing world with Western-style environmental standards is to condemn its citizens to a longer stay in the poverty they wish to escape and would appear to replicate the paternalistic colonialism that anti-globalists decry. As former Mexican president Ernesto Zedillo put it: "A peculiar alliance has recently come into life. Forces from the extreme left, the extreme right, environmentalist groups, trade unions of developed countries and some self-appointed representatives of civil society are gathering around a common endeavor: to save the people of developing countries from—development."

One further benefit of free trade is that it promotes international peace. Countries that trade with one another create mutual interdependence, which raises the cost of armed conflict. If one country depends on another for cheap goods and services, what gain is there to a military invasion? Where interdependence is the nature of the relationship, fates are tied and war makes little sense. International conflict flows out of the sort of nationalism that results from restrictions on free trade. Just as democracies do not go to war with other democracies, so it is that countries with open trading relationships do not go to war. Peace and free trade have a long and storied history, and the very same thinkers who have argued for free trade, and have been excoriated for it by the antimilitarist left, did so because they believed it would promote international harmony and peace. The critics of free trade need to re-read both economic history and the history of ideas, and realize that their opposition to free trade is likely to *increase* international military activity, not reduce it. . . .

Progress Comes from Good Policies

All sides involved in the globalization issue need to take a step back and recognize that a country's "external" policies (its policies concerning international trade and relations) are only half the equation. Free trade is necessary but not sufficient for development. A country's "internal" policies (regulation, monetary stability, and reliable political institutions) are at least as important for economic development. A country open to international trade but with highly restricted markets, high rates of inflation, weak legal and financial institutions, and political instability is unlikely to grow because it is not an attractive place even for those who can relocate there. An agenda for encouraging the spread of wealth to all humanity should support freedom not only across national borders but within them as well. Restrictions on free trade are no more noxious than misguided economic policies put in place by postcolonial leaders, who imported those ideas from economically ill-informed Western elites. The fight to reduce human poverty must take place on many fronts.

Despite their attempts to monopolize it, the anti-globalists' views are not the only ones to lay a legitimate claim to the word "progressive." The more than 200-year-long attempt to open up the world to the free flow of goods, services, and people, and to make the wealth of the West available to the rest of the world, is one of the most progressive projects in human history. It has already resulted in previously unimaginable increases in wealth in those parts of the world most open to trade, and there is no reason to believe those benefits will not be extended to those who have yet to experience them.

Those who wish to slow down, stop, or politically control that process are the true reactionaries, standing atop the wave of human progress yelling "stop" simply because they cannot understand how an uncontrolled, spontaneously ordered process can possibly benefit everyone. Progress is not synonymous with intentional human control. Progress comes from good policies that let individuals use their local knowledge to their own benefit, and in doing so, unintentionally benefit others. The path toward development requires free trade. To restrict it is to condemn to prolonged poverty those who most need to escape it.

| *"The era of globalisation has resulted in slower economic and social progress."*

Globalization Does Not Benefit Developing Nations

Dave Curran

Dave Curran argues in the following viewpoint that studies showing a link between trade liberalization and prosperity are misleading. Trade, he contends, does not automatically lead to development; rather, trade is a by-product of development. He points out that the most economically liberalized nations experience less growth than nations with only moderately liberalized markets. Admitting that trade is an important steppingstone for developing nations to become industrialized and integrated with the global community, he calls for intergovernmental organizations to temper capitalist greed with common morality. Curran is deputy president of the Union of Students in Ireland, an organization dedicated to expanding opportunities for higher education.

As you read, consider the following questions:

1. How many people worldwide, as Curran reports, suffer chronic undernourishment?

Dave Curran, "Rigged Rules and Diminished Progress: The Failure of Globalisation," Indymedia Ireland, November 21, 2004. Reproduced by permission of the author.

2. By what measures can human well-being be determined, as stated by the author?

3. According to Curran, by what means do developing countries try to "attract multinational corporations"?

The free market solution to world poverty has failed, so countries should be allowed self-determination in their economic policies.

The current religion among much of the economics community is that "openness" to international trade is the best—indeed the only—route out of poverty for the world's poor countries. This chorus echoing the wondrous ability of free trade globalisation to reduce the obscene levels of poverty in the world today has been backed up by the dominant powers that shape the global economy—institutions like the International Monetary Fund [IMF] the World Bank and the OECD [Organization for Economic Cooperation and Development], and powerful rich country governments in North America and Europe. And yet, the past twenty-five years have seen unprecedented levels of rapid economic "liberalisation" on every continent, and at the end of this period half the world still lives on less than two dollars a day and 800 million people are still chronically undernourished.

The 1980s, which saw the beginning of "rolling back" the state in Latin America and Africa under the IMF's "Structural Adjustment Programmes", is now considered by many development agencies to be a "lost decade" in terms of poverty reduction, with economic development slowing in most regions of the world, and with many countries falling back further into poverty. And the 1990s have not been much better. A study by the US-based Centre for Economic and Policy Research found that by all measures of human well-being—infant mortality, life expectancy, even economic growth—progress has been slower in the 1980s and 90s than in previous decades, and in the regions subject to neo-liberal economic policies the most, such as Latin America and Africa, growth has been almost zero, with many countries actually experiencing negative growth. In other words, the era of globalisation has resulted in slower economic and social progress, even by its own narrowly defined indicators. Contrary to the assurances of the World Bank and free-market globalisers, the "rising tide" has lifted mainly yachts, and many boats are now sinking fast.

Free Trade Myths

It is not that there has been no growth under globalisation—rather, that the benefit of this growth has gone primarily to a small few. Inequality in most countries has increased to levels never seen before, and hundreds of millions of poor people have seen their situations worsen. The rabid anti-statism of neo-liberal theory saw African countries instructed to cut back on state expenditure on health care and education. In a region now devastated by AIDS, these recommendations were irresponsible in the extreme.

Despite the failures of the neo-liberal model to reduce poverty, it still remains the dominant discourse among the forces that shape the global economic system. Advocates of neo-liberal globalisation, including the myriad of right-wing "think-tanks" that have come to dominate the political landscape over the past few decades (with generous help from the corporate community), still cling to several discredited myths about the benefits of rapid liberalisation.

One such myth is reinforced by studies of "Global Economic Freedom", which allege to show a strong correlation between "globalising" countries and rich countries. The richest countries, they say, are those that trade more and are more "open" to the global economy. Thus, opening up by cutting back the state and embracing the free market will lead to growth and development. The problem here is one of confused methodology, because economic "openness" has two

Deregulation and the Poor

Evidence of the trends in global poverty and inequality tends not to support the stance taken by proponents of the global liberalization agenda. Gains in poverty reduction [since the 1980s], if any, were relatively small and geographically isolated. The number of poor people rose from 1987 to 1998, and the share of poor people increased in many countries; in 1998 close to half of the population were considered poor in many parts of the world. Moreover, the numbers show that income inequality between and within countries increased along with deregulation of trade and capital markets. In 1980, median income in the richest 10 percent of countries was 77 times greater than in the poorest 10 percent; by 1999, that gap had grown to 122 times. Inequality has also increased within a vast majority of countries.

Christian E. Weller and Adam Hersh,
ZEI Working Paper B02-14, 2002.

very different meanings. Openness can refer to an economic outcome—such as if a country's economy consists largely of imports and exports—or it can refer to government policies of "opening up", which usually involve rapid export increase and deregulation of markets. What the studies that claim to show a link between government policies of "opening up" and prosperity actually show is that as countries get richer, they begin to open up. Development leads to trade, and not the other way around.

For example, a recent Oxfam report entitled "Rigged Rules and Double Standards" studies developing countries that embraced "openness"—defined as following neo-liberal doctrine and dismantling state regulation of the economy. These countries are the ones that rapidly privatised state firms, deregulated financial markets, cut state support of infant industries and suppressed unions in order to drive down wages and attract multinational corporations. When these policies are tested, according to the Oxfam report, "the World Bank view appears as an upside version of reality." It turns out that some of the most successful countries "are anything but rapid liberalisers, while many of the most radical liberalisers have actually achieved very little in terms of economic growth and poverty reduction". For example, South Korea and Taiwan—the very models of successful economic development—achieved growth by ignoring the policy prescriptions of neo-liberals and using massive protectionism and state regulation of the economy. They embraced trade, but very carefully and with strict state guidance. At the other extreme, according to a report by the United Nations Conference on Trade and Development (UNCTAD) in 2004, countries which simply threw open their economies, such as Haiti, are some of the poorest in the world.

Poverty and Trade Systems

While poor countries cannot simply trade their way out of poverty, trade if used correctly can be a powerful force for prosperity and poverty reduction. But the current trade rules are totally unfair, and serve to divert the potential benefits of trade away from the poor and toward the rich and powerful. Trade is not free when all the rules have been rigged to benefit western corporations. Poor farmers in Africa cannot "freely" bargain over price with giant coffee conglomerates, because of the huge bargaining power of the companies and the vulnerability of the producers. And a trading system that values the "intellectual property" of drug companies over the lives of AIDS victims should be either reformed or dismantled. For trade to work for the poor, it must be more than free. It must also be fair trade, and must be combined with redistribution, regulation of capital flight, debt cancellation, environmental sustainability and the dismantling of exploitative power relations. The neo-liberal prescription for development, because it ignores all these considerations, is a shallow, self-serving way of redistributing the world's resources further into the hands of the powerful.

But while free market fundamentalism is a false dawn of world development, its polar extreme is no better. The UNCTAD [United Nations Conference on Trade and Development] report earlier [in 2004] showed that the poorest countries in the world are on the one hand those that are most open, and on the other hand those that close themselves off to the global economy. It seems that grand theories, from either left or right have failed. Just as the crumbling of the Berlin Wall revealed for the world the failures of communism, the defiant chants of protestors from Seattle to Caracas have drowned out the authoritarian mantra that "there is no alternative" to free market capitalism.

The message for poor countries should be that they do have a choice over which socio-economic path to take. There is no single theory or grand narrative which can solve the problems of world poverty. There are many paths, and there are always alternatives. The message of the global justice movement is that we in the rich countries also have a choice. We can allow globalisation to continue to work for the few, rather than the many. Or we can join together with the progressive movements in the global south and forge a new model of inclusive globalisation, one based not on corporate greed but on the principles of equality, solidarity and social justice.

"As trade, foreign investment and technology have spread, the gap between
economic haves and have-nots has frequently widened."

Globalization Promotes Income Inequality

Bob Davis, John Lyons, and Andrew Batson

In the following viewpoint, Wall Street Journal *reporters Bob Davis, John Lyons, and Andrew Batson argue that globalization has led to increasing income inequality worldwide. They suggest that the increasing disparity in Latin America may result from the region's slow growth, while the disparity in China may result from employers seeking out well-educated workers with rare job skills. The authors point out that although the standard of living has generally improved in developing countries such as Mexico, the elite class has seen a disproportionate share of economic growth, leading to widespread political discontent. According to the authors, the scarcity of educational opportunities perpetuates an ever-growing force of unemployed workers who desperately compete for low-paying jobs without benefits.*

Bob Davis, John Lyons, and Andrew Batson, "Globalization's Gains Come with a Price: While Poor Benefit, Inequality Feeds a Backlash Overseas," *Wall Street Journal*, vol. 249, May 24, 2007, pp. A1, A12. Copyright © 2007 by Dow Jones & Company, Inc. Republished with permission of Wall Street Journal, conveyed through Copyright Clearance Center, Inc.

As you read, consider the following questions:

1. How do Davis, Lyons, and Batson define globalization?

2. What increase in per-capita income did the richest 10 percent of urban Chinese households gain between 2000 and 2005, as stated by the authors?

3. According to the authors, how many Mexican textile jobs with health benefits were lost from 2000 to 2007?

A decade ago [in the late nineties], the globalization of commerce promised to be a boon to low-wage workers in developing nations. As wealthy nations shed millions of jobs making apparel, electronics, and other goods, economists predicted that low-skilled workers in Latin America and Asia would benefit because there would be greater demand for their labor—and better wages.

In some ways, globalization delivered as promised. But there was an unexpected consequence. As trade, foreign investment and technology have spread, the gap between economic haves and have-nots has frequently widened, not only in wealthy countries like the U.S. but in poorer ones like Mexico as well. Many economists now say that the biggest winners by far are those with the education and skills to take advantage of new opportunities, leaving many lagging far behind. Incomes of low-skilled workers may rise, but incomes of skilled workers rise a lot faster.

"While globalization was expected to help the less skilled . . . in developing countries, there is overwhelming evidence that these are generally not better off, at least not relative to workers with higher skill or education levels," write economists Pinelopi Koujianou Goldberg of Yale University and Nina Pavcnik of Dartmouth in the spring [2007] issue of the *Journal of Economic Literature.*

Globalization deserves credit for helping lift many millions out of poverty and for improving standards of living of low-wage families. In developing countries around the world, globalization—defined as trading and participating in the global economy—has created a vibrant middle class that has elevated the standards of living for hundreds of millions of people. That's particularly true in China, where the incomes of low-skilled workers have consistently risen. The poor in countries like Vietnam and elsewhere in Southeast Asia have also benefited greatly since those countries have opened their economies. In many developing countries around the world, life expectancies and health care have improved, as have educational opportunities.

But because globalization is also creating more inequality, it is raising questions about how much inequality countries can bear and whether these gaps could ultimately produce a backlash that will undermine trade and investment liberalization around the world.

Rising Inequality

Many developing nations seem to be following in the footsteps of the U.S., where the income gap has grown sharply since the early 1970s. A 2006 study of Latin America, a region long marked by profound gaps between rich and poor, by World Bank economists Guillermo Perry and Marcelo Olarreaga found that the income divide deepened after economic liberalization in nine of the 12 countries examined.

While that could partly be explained by Latin America's slow rate of economic growth, income gaps are widening in fast-growing Asian nations as well, including Thailand and India. It's even grown [since the late 1990s] in South Korea, a country long known for an egalitarian commitment to education.

Then there's China. One of the fastest-growing economies in the world has generated significant wage gains for its rank and file. Yet income inequality is also growing because of the huge gains being posted by the upper crust. Between 1984 and

Globalization and Poverty

In Latin America, globalization has a mixed record as a poverty fighter. In China, there has been a widespread reduction in poverty since the country opened its economy.

Latin America

Bottom quintile's average income*, change from before to after economic liberalization

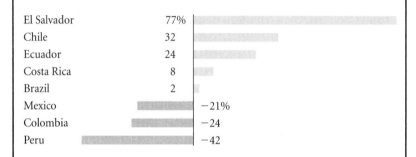

El Salvador	77%
Chile	32
Ecuador	24
Costa Rica	8
Brazil	2
Mexico	−21%
Colombia	−24
Peru	−42

China

Population living on less than $1 a day

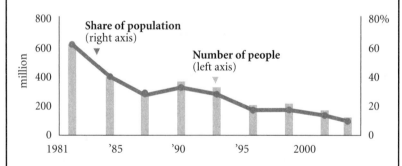

*In constant 1985 dollars, purchasing power parity, derived from several years before and after trade liberalization in each country

TAKEN FROM: Bob Davis, John Lyons, and Andrew Batson, "Globalization's Gains Come with a Price," *Wall Street Journal*, May 24, 2007.

2004, China's income inequality as measured by the Gini index—zero is perfect equality and 100 is perfect inequality—increased to 47 from 29, according to World Bank researchers Martin Ravallion and Shaohua Chen. From 2000 to 2005, per-capita income of the bottom 10% of urban households in China rose 26% while those at the top saw gains of 133%.

While Mexico hasn't experienced the spectacular growth of China, wages of low-skilled workers have improved [from 2003 to 2007]. Since 2000, the percentage of Mexicans living in poverty has fallen below 20% for the first time ever in the nation's history.

Even so, skilled workers in Mexico still earn far more, relative to unskilled workers, than they did before liberalization. In 2004, those in the top 10th percentile earned 4.7 times more than those in the bottom 10th, compared with four times as much in 1987, according to Columbia University economists Eric Verhoogen and Kensuke Teshima.

By other measures, income inequality is far greater. The World Bank, for instance, estimates that the top 10% of Mexicans accounted for 39% of the country's total spending in 2004, while the bottom 10% accounted for less than 2%.

Growing Discontent

The benefits of globalization have elevated the standards of living for hundreds of millions of people. Yet the consequences of widening income inequality are also profound. Those without much education or skills often find themselves stuck in jobs in the underground economy that don't pay health-care or pension benefits. That's boosted immigration to better-off regions domestically or to the U.S. and Europe, where anti-immigrant sentiment is surging.

Growing inequality also feeds the populist argument that globalization is a sucker's game that benefits only the elites.

In Latin America, that sense of alienation has powered populist presidential candidates who won in Ecuador, Bolivia,

Nicaragua and Venezuela and came close to carrying Mexico [in 2006]. In China, the ruling Communist Party worries that support for liberalization could crumble. The government needs to "safeguard social fairness and justice and ensure that all of the people share in the fruits of reform and development," said Chinese Premier Wen Jiabao in March [2007].

How does globalization boost inequality? The question is too fresh to have definitive answers, but it's clear that international competition forces local firms to add skilled workers who can handle newer technology and shed workers who can't. Foreign firms bring new technology to developing nations and boost demand there for skilled workers by paying 10% to 20% more than domestic firms, says Dirk Willem te Velde, a research fellow at the Overseas Development Institute, a United Kingdom think tank.

Access to education also plays an important role. Developing nations rarely crank out enough college-trained workers to match growing demand, boosting the wages for fresh graduates. Unskilled workers who get laid off can't find retraining and add to the pool of workers looking for low-wage work. . . .

Part of Mexico's problem is that U.S. manufacturers looking for bargain prices have rerouted orders to China, where wages are even lower. Cobitel [a towel company in Puebla, Mexico,] had to cut payroll after a big South Carolina textile customer shifted orders to China in 2004. Overall, Mexican textile jobs that pay health benefits, which peaked at 195,000 in 2000, fell by one-third to 127,000 [in 2007], according to Labor Ministry statistics.

But China's success doesn't fully explain the puzzle of growing global income inequality. If it did, China's low-wage workers would have seen especially fast growth in income, reducing income inequality. While low-wage workers have benefited, it's elite workers that have benefited most. In part, that's because the companies in China doing work for overseas markets usually look for a set of skills few Chinese have, such as foreign-language fluency and technical knowledge.

Migration of the Working Class

Investment by Japanese and Korean companies has transformed the coastal city of Dalian, as crumbling slums and boarded-up factories have given way to new shopping malls and fancy apartment complexes. But the accompanying surge in real-estate prices has made Dalian nearly unaffordable for lower-paid locals, who often complain they are being literally pushed out of the city.

"The fact that ordinary people in Dalian can't afford to buy a house in the city center is indisputable. The city government should reflect on this," one Dalian resident using the name Mu Fan wrote in a comment on a government-sponsored Web site.

Such social tensions have become an increasing political problem for the Communist Party, whose legitimacy rests on its ability to deliver a broad improvement in the populace's standard of living. Wary of being identified as favoring an urban elite, leaders have [in 2007] expanded social programs for the poorest and campaigned against wealthy people who flout tax and family-planning laws.

Expanded education can ease inequality, as more workers qualify for skilled jobs. In Mexico, the income gap has diminished somewhat since 2000, partly reflecting improved education levels. Since 2000, for instance, Puebla State Popular Autonomous University, a large private university, has added undergraduate degrees in such specialties as bionics, electronics and software and is planning to add degrees in biotechnology, power-grid administration and plastics.

Another major factor: So many Poblanos [residents of Puebla] have given up on their home turf and migrated to the U.S. that competition has eased somewhat for lower-skilled jobs. The greater number of Poblanos working abroad has also increased the amount of cash being sent back home, boosting the incomes of many residents. In the past decade, New York has become a magnet for many Poblanos, so much so that mole poblano, a Puebla specialty, is now widely available for sale in the borough of Queens.

Mr. Flores, [a Poblano who lost his job due to globalization], has two brothers who have decamped for the U.S. but says he doesn't want to follow suit because he doesn't want to leave his wife and daughter. Instead, Mr. Flores is looking for work as a day laborer, building homes for Puebla's surging new middle class. "I have a fight in front of me trying to find work," he says.

> "The effects on inequality due to foreign investment and capital market liberalization, while not minor, were much smaller than the effects of technology transfers."

Globalization Is Not Solely to Blame for Income Inequality

Gary Becker

In response to a 2007 International Monetary Fund report's suggestion that income growth in developing countries favors those whose incomes are already relatively high, Gary Becker postulates that the richer and more educated citizens of developing nations receive a disproportionate share of economic increase because they are often more proficient with technology, giving them access to higher paying jobs. In the following viewpoint, he asserts that extending educational opportunities to the poorest members of developing nations would lead to more productivity and widespread prosperity. Becker is a professor of economics at the University of Chicago Booth School of Business and a recipient of the Alfred Nobel Memorial Prize in Economics for his work in microeconomics.

Gary Becker, "Globalization and Inequality," Becker-Posner Blog, October 14, 2007. Reproduced by permission.

As you read, consider the following questions:

1. As described by Becker, how does international trade theory predict higher wages for unskilled workers in an increasingly globalized world?

2. According to the author, how has technology transfer intensified the income gap in developing nations?

3. Despite the growing disparity of wealth, how does Becker assert the poor in developing nations have benefited from globalization?

A [2007] report . . . issued . . . by the IMF [International Monetary Fund] . . . shows that greater globalization during the past two decades contributed significantly to rising inequality during this period in most developing as well as developed countries. The media greeted this conclusion about the connection between inequality and globalization with claims that the new report is "handing critics of globalization a powerful weapon" and "The report is an unusual admission by the IMF of the downsides of globalization" (*Wall Street Journal*). Yet a careful evaluation of the report's findings on income and inequality provides in most respects an optimistic assessment of the effects of globalization on developing nations.

The report analyzes what happened to incomes and inequality in over 50 countries. It finds that essentially all these countries had large increases in per capita incomes since the early 1980s. While the growth was positive at different income levels, including those at the very bottom, income growth was not uniform among different skills, or at different parts of the income distribution. Incomes grew faster for the more skilled and in higher income quintiles, which implies that various measures of inequality typically increased in developing nations.

A Mixed Blessing

[The] combined contribution [of trade liberalization and financial globalization] to rising inequality has been much lower than that of technological change, both at a global level and especially markedly in developing countries. The spread of technology is, of course, itself related to increased globalization, but technological progress is nevertheless seen to have a separately identifiable effect on inequality. The disequalizing impact of financial openness—mainly felt through foreign direct investment (FDI)—and technological progress appear to be working through similar channels by increasing the premium on higher skills, rather than limiting opportunities for economic advancement. Consistent with this, increased access to education is associated with more equal income distributions on average.

Florence Jaumotte, Subir Lall, and Chris Papageorgiou,
IMF Working Paper 08/185, July 2008.

Three Effects of Globalization

To explain these results, the IMF authors divide the effects of greater globalization into expanded world trade, greater foreign investment, and increased transfers of modern technologies. They find that all three dimensions of globalization tended to increase per capita incomes of both developing as well as developed countries. International trade theory implies that trade by a poorer country would increase the relative earnings of its lower skilled workers because richer countries want products from poorer countries that use relatively large quantities of unskilled workers, such as textiles. The report's evidence quite strongly supports this building block of trade theory: greater trade alone would have lowered earnings inequality within developing countries.

However, the most powerful effect on inequality from globalization is due to transfers of modern technologies. The evidence from developed economies has been that modern technologies, like the computer and Internet, favor more educated and other skilled workers; in economic parlance, that these technologies are skill biased. This effect of technological progress has been used to explain the sharply rising gap in earnings between college graduates and others during the past three decades in the United States. Not surprisingly, the IMF's study finds that a similar skill bias applies to international technology transfers, that they raised the earnings gap between more skilled and less skilled workers in developing countries. In other words, foreign direct investment has a skill bias too, so that its sharp growth over the past 25 years raised inequality in developing countries. Better capital markets had a similar effect on inequality. However, the evidence in this report indicates that the effects on inequality due to foreign investment and capital market liberalization, while not minor, were much smaller than the effects of technology transfers.

Education Alleviates Poverty

Is this greater gap between the earnings of more and less skilled workers a good or bad result of globalization? Let us accept that greater inequality is not good, other things the same, but other things are different in the IMF results on inequality. The increased earnings gap between persons with more and less education in developing countries reflects that the earnings of more educated individuals rose faster than the earnings of the less educated. The IMF report clearly shows that generally the poorer and less educated in developing nations also became better off in that they have more to spend on food, shelter, health, automobiles, and the other goods that they desire. This improvement in well-being at the lower end of the income distribution surely should count as a benefit of globalization.

The larger earnings gap by education essentially means that the returns on investments in schooling increased. Few critics of globalization would claim that its effects were bad if globalization significantly raised the returns to financial or physical capital owned by local investors in developing countries. So how can one complain that globalization is bad because it raises the returns on the education of local human capital investors? Higher returns to human capital investments as well as greater returns to plant and equipment mean that the economy is more productive, which should be a welcome development to poorer as well as richer countries.

Yet intellectuals and politicians in many countries of Latin America, Africa, and even parts of Asia have heavily criticized globalization and its effects. I believe that developing countries in which the criticisms are strongest are generally countries that have done a bad job of educating [their] population[s]. Higher returns on investments in education and other human capital are small comfort to the children of poor families who often do not have easy access to secondary schools, let alone to universities and other forms of advanced investments in human capital. The lesson of the IMF report and other studies is that globalization is not the source of these serious problems. Rather, the lesson is that many developing countries have to do much more to open up access to better and greater education for children coming from lower income families. Only then would these families be able to take advantage of the higher returns to education produced by greater trade and the inflow into their economies of modern technologies and foreign capital.

> "The rules that govern world markets have disrupted the much larger share of food production that is for domestic markets."

Globalization Is Worsening the Food Crisis

Sophia Murphy

Sophia Murphy is a senior advisor at the Institute for Agriculture and Trade Policy. In the following viewpoint, she argues that free trade has contributed to the food crisis. Murphy states that countries that do not produce enough food to meet citizens' needs are hardest hit by fluctuating prices, as other nations raise export taxes in an effort to keep scarce food within their own borders. According to the author, trade liberalization has perpetuated developing nations' dependency on food imports, as governments have given up protectionist policies designed to bolster domestic food production. Murphy suggests that agricultural reform within nations has greater potential to alleviate the food crisis than international organizations and trade agreements.

Sophia Murphy, "Will Free Trade Solve the Food Crisis?" *Food Ethics*, vol. 3, Summer 2008, pp. 21–22. Reproduced by permission.

As you read, consider the following questions:

1. At least how many countries took steps to lower the price of imported food, as noted by Murphy?

2. According to the author, what problems have contributed to the current food crisis?

3. What additional benefits does Murphy believe developing countries can reap while increasing agricultural productivity?

Hardly a day has passed in the past few months [in the summer of 2008] when high food prices, and the political and humanitarian consequences of those prices, have not been in the news.

A flurry of tariff reductions has greeted the crisis. The World Bank reports that at least 24 countries have reduced tariffs and/or value-added taxes on imports. Yet even as the tariffs fall, some governments in the major exporting countries have imposed or raised export taxes on food commodity exports.

An April briefing from the International Food Policy Research Institute lists Argentina, Bolivia, Cambodia, China, Egypt, Ethiopia, India, Indonesia, Kazakhstan, Mexico, Morocco, Russia, Thailand, Ukraine, Venezuela, and Vietnam as countries that have restricted food exports, imposed price controls on food, or both. Trade economists' ideal of a single world market requires both importers and exporters to be ready to trade at all times, regardless of political pressures at home. In the real world, of course, this is impossible. Governments must at least be seen to be doing everything possible to protect their people from hunger, regardless of trade obligations.

Some analysts have used the crisis to argue in favour of the conclusion of the Doha Agenda [a World Trade Organization summit held in Doha, Qatar]. With tariffs falling anyway, and the need for income support programmes reduced by high world prices, the moment is judged propitious to lock in changes through new multilateral trade rules. Given the experience of the past decade, such confidence is bewildering.

Undermining State Protections

Further opening up agricultural markets is likely to increase volatility of agricultural prices. At the national level, governments' ability to support agricultural production using direct interventions in markets has been significantly reduced over the past two decades. Structural adjustment programmes and international trade agreements have curtailed governments' ability to manage commodity production and trade. Tools previously available to help increase production in times of scarcity, to even out supply between bountiful and less good years, or to help producers adapt to changing production constraints, are more expensive or banned under existing trade and investment agreements.

Trade liberalisation and the neglect of domestic agriculture have increased the dependence of net food importing developing countries on food imports. Today, these countries pay more than ever for the food they import to meet their populations' needs. World markets in many crops remain a small fraction of total production yet the rules that govern world markets have disrupted the much larger share of food production that is for domestic markets.

Rather than establishing fairer markets, multilateral trade rules have strengthened the position of the most powerful players in the food system, particularly transnational agribusinesses. These firms have thrived on market deregulation. In many places, they have pushed small and diversified growers out of the markets in their bid to establish stable and homogenous suppliers for their processors. Cargill [an international food producer] announced in April [2008] that third quarter profits rose 86% to US$1.03 billion.

Increased Instability

At the April 2008 spring meetings of the IMF [International Monetary Fund] and World Bank, the WTO [World Trade Organization] Director General, Pascal Lamy, said, "In this period of increased financial uncertainty around the world, the rules-based trading system of the WTO provides a hugely important source of economic stability for governments, for business and for consumers".

Yet the global food crisis is a clear example of how the rules have failed. The Doha Agenda is not the answer. The WTO has no mandate even to discuss, let alone tackle, the major sources of uncertainty in the food system. In the following list of problems causing rapid food inflation—climate change, natural resource depletion, the quadrupling of oil prices, the lack of competition in world commodity markets, speculation on commodity exchanges, the rapid expansion of biofuels production, hoarding supplies—the WTO has nothing to say or actually worsens the problem with its rules pushing deregulation and increased international trade.

However many WTO rules there are in the world, they won't hold when a crisis really hits. How did Malawi pull out of chronic food shortages? By ignoring the advice of its creditors (particularly the World Bank) and reintroducing subsidies to fertilizers, so as to boost production. Global trade benefits immeasurably from clear, strong rules. All commercial transactions do. But those rules have to pay attention to social, environmental and political realities or they cannot last.

Most food trade takes place within national borders. World supply and demand have a powerful impact in these local markets, but the influence is effectively one-way. Governments must respond to the food crisis responsibly, and with due attention to multilateral concerns. Many of the world's hungriest people depend on traded food for their next meal. But it is just as important that trade imperatives do not drive the debate. Strengthening domestic production and building resilient local markets should provide the building blocks for larger national, regional and global markets.

For agriculture, as for other sectors, the WTO has failed to provide the stability that is so evidently lacking in today's food markets. The key to stability in food is public stocks, which are a whole lot more certain and predictable than the wave of export restrictions newly imposed in the face of popular protests in a number of countries. The world market in many foods is residual: most production is not traded anyway. If exporters then decide to limit or ban exports, the price shocks are magnified for importers, most of whom can ill-afford sudden price increases.

Possible Solutions

An international panel of 400 or so contributors, meeting under UN auspices, released their report, the International Assessment of Agricultural Science and Technology for Development or IAASTD, on 15th April [2008]. In brief, the report calls for radical changes to modern agriculture to meet the challenges of hunger, climate change and increasingly fragile and eroded ecosystems.

The first step for governments should be to shape trade according to their country's collective preferences. This requires enlarging national policy space, not least over trade and investment rules. Governments' trade obligations should be determined by their commitments to protect and promote human rights, including the right to food, and to their commitments under environmental agreements, such as the Convention on Biological Diversity and Framework Convention on Climate Change.

The second objective should be to raise productivity, especially in Africa, where the potential gains, and need, are greatest. This does not mean fertiliser applications and more hybrid seeds, at least not at the core. It means redefining productivity to look at food output per acre rather than yield

Growing Food for Export

[Since 1996], the World Bank and the World Trade Organization encouraged developing countries to switch from growing food for domestic markets to growing cash crops for export to industrial countries. Traditional African food crops like sorghum, cassava, yams and millet are not traded internationally, so they typically were ignored by international agribusinesses and globalization proponents. Instead, farmers were encouraged to grow crops like coffee, sugar, cocoa beans, tea and cotton and then use the export earnings to purchase food, often low-priced imports from industrial countries. Globalization cheerleaders viewed food self-sufficiency as obsolete. Although imported food benefited consumers in the developing world when prices were low, local farmers were often displaced by low-priced imports. Now that imported food prices are rising, consumers cannot afford sustenance and there is too little local production to provide food for local markets in many countries.

Food & Water Watch,
"What's Behind the Global Food Crisis?" July 2008.

per plant, and investing in ecologically sound and socially just technologies. This will require public investment and planning, including in post-harvest storage, roads, and communications infrastructure. Developing countries should focus on opportunities to build local capital flows, to generate local jobs and maximize the potential 'spill-over' benefits in processing and services industries.

Third, public stocks need to be re-established, with planning for local, national and regional roles. Such stocks provide an important buffer against price spikes and food insecurity.

Despite their cost (real and in lost theoretical market efficiency) they are an important strategy, especially for countries whose food security has come to rely on world markets. The world market will function better with the stability that well-managed stocks can provide.

Fourth, disciplines to curb speculative activity in food markets should be explored. Trading in commodities-derived financial instruments make prices more volatile. Volatile prices hurt producers and consumers alike. Regulations to control derivatives are essential if futures and options are to provide a usable risk management tool for producers and processors. Buyers should be able to manage price risks by purchasing futures contracts that have a transparent relation to real supplies. Farmers and smaller commodities buyers cannot afford to use futures contracts to manage price risks when commodities exchange prices are too heavily affected by speculative investors.

Fifth, bioenergy policies need to be designed so as not to undermine food security or the environment. Governments, especially in the largest energy-consuming countries, need to pursue energy security based on a substantial reduction of their energy use. This requires a reorganisation of economies, including the agriculture sector, away from heavy dependence on fossil fuels and towards locally integrated markets.

These changes are not just possible; they are essential to the continuing viability of our food and agriculture system. The price crisis offers us the opportunity to re-engage the public sector in deliberate and far-sighted investment in ecologically sound and socially just outcomes. Let's face it— would you like the market to decide whether you eat tonight?

> *"Demand and prices for food are rising, so freeing trade would be the best remedy for the world's poor."*

Globalization Can Solve the Food Crisis

Caroline Boin and Alec van Gelder

In the following viewpoint, Caroline Boin and Alec van Gelder argue that trade barriers have caused food prices to soar, especially in developing nations. The authors maintain that interventionist policies of African countries have discouraged food production, contributing to the undernourishment of millions. Abolishing tariffs and quotas, they contend, would increase agricultural efficiency, alleviate the high prices that mark the food crisis, and allow the hardest-hit nations to invest in new yield-increasing technologies. Boin is a research fellow in the environment program at the International Policy Network in London, where van Gelder is the network director.

As you read, consider the following questions:

1. If food prices rise 30 percent over five years, how does Gary Becker, as cited by the authors, predict living standards will be affected in rich and poor countries?

Caroline Boin and Alec Van Gelder, "Free Trade Can Stop World Food Crisis Turning into a Tragedy," *The Scotsman*, April 19, 2008. Reproduced by permission.

2. What are Africa's most costly deviations from free trade, according to the World Bank's estimate cited by the authors?

3. According to Boin and van Gelder, what percent of the African workforce is employed in the agriculture industry?

Protectionism has failed people in poor countries, but getting rid of tariffs will boost production and cut prices. Rising food prices have caused street protests from Mexico to India to Senegal. But this could be a blessing in disguise if it makes governments eliminate the trade barriers that exacerbate high prices: the poorest countries will benefit most from dropping their own tariffs.

Nobel economics laureate Gary Becker estimates that a 30 per cent rise in food prices over five years would cause living standards to fall by 3 per cent in rich countries and by more than 20 per cent in poor countries.

A few countries have already temporarily eased tariffs on agricultural imports to soften the blow for consumers—even the European Union. Thailand is considering a cut of 50 per cent for maize, soy beans and other animal feed.

These tariff reductions will offset price increases, not just by lowering prices, but by increasing supply. Increased trade in agricultural goods (not just food) could even help avert famine where produce is subject to intense government control, such as in North Korea, Ethiopia, Kenya and many others. But many countries resist free trade in food, domestically or with neighbours.

In Africa, 200 million people are underfed, according to the United Nations Food and Agriculture Organisation. They have borne the brunt of counterproductive state management of agriculture that has damaged farmers and economies.

For years, governments in Africa forced farmers to surrender their crops to state-run marketing boards at below market rates. Some of these corrupt and inefficient institutions have been weakened or abolished but many other restrictions on agriculture remain, including tariffs on produce and on inputs such as fertiliser and machinery—and even on exports.

Tariffs Hurt Developing Nations

Many development analysts are obsessed with subsidies paid to farmers in rich countries, now extended to biofuels, and the damage it inflicts on the world's poor. But it is the world's poorest countries that impose the highest barriers to trade with each other: agricultural exports between sub-Saharan countries face an average tariff of 33.6 per cent, the highest of any region. A whopping 70 per cent of the world's trade barriers are imposed by governments in poor countries on people in other poor countries.

Alhaji Ahmed Abdulkadir, a presidential adviser in Nigeria, has said: "I can assure you that my pen is always ready to ban more items as long as they are available in Nigeria." These would be "either banned completely, and where we have doubts, we will impose high tariffs".

Nigeria's import bans have included staples such as rice, maize and vegetable oil, making its people pay sky-high prices. The World Bank estimates global free trade in all goods would add £144 billion to world income each year, half of that going to poor countries.

Sixty-three per cent of that immediate gain would come from freeing agricultural trade alone. In African countries, nearly all of that 63 per cent would come from removing their own import tariffs and quotas, which artificially restrict access to other markets, including their neighbours'. High food prices are a clear and immediate reason to cut tariffs, but that does not mean it will happen.

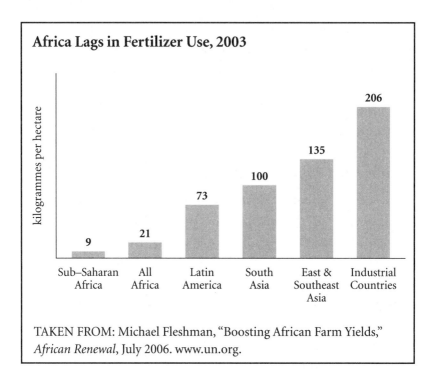

Africa Lags in Fertilizer Use, 2003

TAKEN FROM: Michael Fleshman, "Boosting African Farm Yields," *African Renewal*, July 2006. www.un.org.

The Failure of Protectionism

For decades, protectionism has been imposed against the interests of local consumers, because of an unholy coalition of western activists and local vested interests.

Trade barriers of any kind, including "green" subsidies, tariffs and quotas, harm both consumers and producers. They artificially increase costs, leading to unnecessary waste of scarce natural and human resources. Consumers and producers spend more to purchase the same goods and services, so have less to invest in new technologies or to save for the future.

Although some claim that trade barriers would help the environment, they are actually counterproductive. They favour the status quo by rewarding inefficient producers and thus delaying the adoption of cleaner, resource-saving technologies.

India demonstrates the follies of protectionism. Until 1984, India had one car manufacturer, which produced just one car—the Ambassador—which was technologically inferior, belched pollutants and was unaffordable to all but the elite. In 1984, India began to open its market to foreign car producers. This process exploded after the reforms of 1991, and millions of Indians have benefited from competition, purchasing cars that are less expensive, cleaner, more technologically advanced and efficient.

Under the slogan "Make Trade Fair", groups such as Oxfam and Christian Aid claim that protecting local industries and agriculture with tariffs will allow them to grow and become competitive—with local consumers, especially the poorest, suffering higher prices. But decades of protectionism have done little for sub-Saharan Africa.

Fertilizer Use Drops in Africa

It is no surprise that crop yields—like income and life expectancy—have steadily decreased across much of Africa since the 1980s. The technologies that could turn their fortunes around, such as fertiliser, irrigation and genetically-modified crops, remain largely out of reach. Worse—and contrary to trends in Asia and Latin America—fertiliser use has actually fallen in many African countries in the past two decades.

Whereas an average of 107kg of fertiliser is used per hectare in the developing world as a whole, African countries use only 8kg. The consequence has been disastrous: 70 per cent of the continent's workforce is still in agriculture, mainly subsistence farming, contributing only about 25 per cent of gross domestic product.

Demand and prices for food are rising, so freeing trade would be the best remedy for the world's poor, cutting prices at a stroke and boosting production. High food prices are putting pressure on protectionist governments to free their trade or face angry mobs. The choice is obvious, lest a crisis turn into a tragedy.

Periodical Bibliography

The following articles have been selected to supplement the diverse views presented in this chapter.

Economist	"The Nuts and Bolts Come Apart," March 26, 2009.
Mark Landler	"Financial Chill May Hit Developing Countries," *New York Times*, September 25, 2008.
David J. Lynch	"Developing Nations Poised to Challenge USA as King of the Hill," *USA Today*, February 8, 2007.
Harold Meyerson	"A Global New Deal," *American Prospect*, December 15, 2008.
Shamarukh Mohiuddin	"Building Trade Capacity in Poor Countries," *Progressive Policy Institute Policy Report*, July 6, 2007.
Robin Moriney	"Who Benefits from Globalization?" *Wall Street Journal*, February 28, 2007.
Floyd Norris	"Maybe Developing Nations Are Not Emerging but Have Emerged," *New York Times*, December 30, 2006.
Nita Rudra	"Globalization and the Strengthening of Democracy in the Developing World," *American Journal of Political Science*, October 2005.
Robert Samuelson	"Will America Pass the Baton?" *Newsweek*, March 6, 2006.
Michael Schuman	"Potholes on the Path to Prosperity," *Time*, January 22, 2009. www.time.com.
Roy C. Smith	"Enterprise Capital in Emerging Markets," *Independent Review*, Summer 2007.
Fareed Zakaria	"The World Bails Us Out," *Newsweek*, February 4, 2008.

OPPOSING
VIEWPOINTS®
SERIES

CHAPTER 4

How Is Globalization Impacting the U.S. Economy?

Chapter Preface

In 1930 Congress passed the Smoot-Hawley Tariff Act, a measure that President Herbert Hoover hoped would raise tariffs on agricultural imports and help American farmers make gains in the faltering economic market. Instead, the act raised import duties on more than twenty thousand products that ranged from agricultural to industrial, leaving the U.S. economy isolated behind a tariff wall that many economists assumed would only aggravate the country's economic woes. Indeed, in response to the new high tariffs, foreign nations enacted their own trade barriers, and U.S. imports and exports were cut nearly in half. Some historians blame this protectionist act for devastating the economy and plunging America into the darkest years of the Great Depression.

The memory of the Smoot-Hawley Act has since pressed U.S. politicians and economists to favor the removal of trade barriers and to embrace an open market policy. The government's support for globalization over the past several decades is evidence of the country's high regard for free trade. However, after America and the globe experienced the onset of a new financial crisis in 2008, the specter of protectionism has returned. Within the economic stimulus bill that Congress offered to President Barack Obama is a clause that stipulated that specific government-sponsored building projects must use U.S. steel instead of imported steel. Several foreign leaders spoke out against the adoption of this clause, suggesting that retaliation might be forthcoming and a new Smoot-Hawley era would prevail. Opposing such a grim future, Jim Flaherty, the finance minister of Canada—a country that exports about $5 billion worth of steel each year to the United States—stated, "What we need to do is avoid the mistakes that were made in the 1930s when countries took the protectionist route, which resulted in a very long recession/depression." Disregarding such warnings, Obama signed the bill into law in February 2009.

Although no global retaliation has been forthcoming over the "Buy American" clause, some recent protectionist measures are sparking heated response. One part of a congressional appropriations bill—the follow-up to the stimulus bill—passed in March 2009 eliminated funding for a pilot program that was to allow Mexican trucking companies to transport goods into the United States. American teamster unions opposed this program, saying it did not take into account U.S. pollution standards or safety regulations. The Mexican government immediately condemned the termination of the program as a violation of the North American Free Trade Agreement, which guarantees that truckers from Mexico and the United States could operate freely in each other's countries. In response, Mexico imposed tariffs on ninety U.S. agricultural and industrial imports. The *Economist* reported that the taxed goods ranged "from strawberries and wine to cordless telephones. The list was carefully chosen to avoid pushing up prices of staples in Mexico while hitting goods that are important exports for a range of American states." Whether this action is a harbinger of a growing protectionist stance is unclear, but many economists see the undermining of free trade as a detrimental policy that could sink the nation—and the world—into another depression.

In the following chapter, two authors carry on the protectionist debate by arguing the necessity of "Buy American" mandates in the current financial crisis. Other commentators in the chapter offer differing opinions on the ways in which globalization has impacted U.S. policy and the government's attempts to protect American jobs while promoting free trade in difficult economic times.

"The members of the U.S. Chamber of Commerce have seen [NAFTA's] benefits firsthand as it has generated new opportunities for workers, farmers, consumers and businesses."

NAFTA Benefits America

John Murphy

John Murphy is vice president of international affairs at the U.S. Chamber of Commerce. In the following viewpoint, Murphy claims that the North American Free Trade Agreement (NAFTA) has benefited the United States by adding to jobs, increasing sales of manufactured goods, and boosting the overall gross domestic product. Murphy insists that NAFTA has also strengthened economic ties between the three North American nations and provided advantages to workers, consumers, and businesses throughout the continent.

As you read, consider the following questions:

1. How many jobs does the author say NAFTA has created in America between its inception in 1994 and December 2007?

John Murphy, "NAFTA at 15: Assessing Its Benefits," Chamber Post, February 18, 2009. Reproduced by permission.

2. According to Murphy, what percent of the new jobs created by NAFTA in America were in small to mid-sized firms?

3. What was the value of U.S. manufactured goods purchased by Canada and Mexico in 2007, as reported by the author?

Since [NAFTA] entered into force in January 1994, rapid growth in trade between the United States, Canada, and Mexico has created significant new opportunities for workers, farmers, consumers and businesses in all three countries. However, despite this 15-year record, many of the agreement's benefits are poorly understood. Below, I address its benefits, debunk some criticisms of the agreement, and place it in proper context.

Increases in Trade

The remarkable results of NAFTA are most obvious in the tripling of U.S. trade with Canada and Mexico over the past 15 years. Trade in goods between the three countries rose from $293 billion in 1993 to just under $1 trillion in 2008. In addition, U.S. exports of services to Canada and Mexico exceed $60 billion annually. Each day, the three North American countries conduct well over $2.5 billion in trade.

In fact, Canada and Mexico are by far the two largest markets in the world for U.S. exports, purchasing more than a third of total exports. U.S. merchandise exports to Canada and Mexico rose from $142 billion in 1993 to a projected $422 billion in 2008. This represents a near tripling in U.S. goods exports to Canada and Mexico (a rise of 197%) in a period when U.S. exports to the rest of the world grew by 141%.

While NAFTA has probably boosted U.S. economic growth in limited ways, it certainly hasn't hurt it. In the 1993–2007 period, U.S. GDP [gross domestic product] grew by 54%, Mexican GDP grew by 48% and Canadian GDP expanded by 56%.

A Decline in Unemployment

While some critics have claimed NAFTA caused the loss of a million U.S. jobs, U.S. employment has risen from 110.7 million in January 1994 to 138.9 million in December 2007. This represents an increase of more than 28 million jobs, or a 25% expansion in the number of Americans working.

At the same time, the U.S. unemployment rate was markedly lower in the years after NAFTA came into force. In the period 1994–2007, it averaged 5.1%. This compares with an average rate of 7.1% during a period of similar length just before NAFTA came into force (1982–1993). While the financial crisis that struck in 2008 has caused unemployment to rise sharply, this has nothing to do with the 15-year-old trade agreement.

Did NAFTA lead to the creation of 28 million jobs or reduce U.S. unemployment rates by two percentage points? No. During a time of dramatic changes in the U.S. economy, the vast majority of economists believe the agreement has had little net effect on the number of jobs. But it has fostered growth in export-oriented jobs over jobs that aren't tied to exports. Jobs tied to exports generally pay 15–20% higher wages than those that aren't, so the shift in the mix of U.S. jobs toward more export-oriented industries represents a net gain for working Americans.

Small and mid-size firms have long been the primary motor of U.S. job creation, accounting for well over half of all new jobs in recent years. Today, more than 110,000 of America's small and mid-size firms export to Canada and Mexico. These small exporters hail from all 50 states. The

NAFTA's True Benefits

Contrary to popular opinion, since its inception NAFTA has generated significant gains for the U.S. Together, Canada and Mexico constitute America's largest trade partner, accounting for about 83 percent of all merchandise trade between the U.S. and our FTA [free trade agreement] partners and 29 percent of all U.S. merchandise trade in 2007. Each day NAFTA countries conduct roughly $2.2 billion in trilateral trade. This trade supports U.S. jobs, bolsters productivity, and promotes investment. Since 1994, U.S. GDP [gross domestic product] grew more than 50 percent in the first 13 years of the agreement, and the economy created a net 26 million new jobs.

Daniella Markheim,
Heritage Foundation Web Memo No. 2116,
October 24, 2008.

states that export the most to Canada and Mexico are Texas, California, Michigan, Ohio, Illinois, New York, Indiana, Pennsylvania, Indiana and Washington.

The dollar value of small-business exports is anything but small. U.S. small and medium-size companies exported $70 billion worth of manufactured goods to Mexico and Canada in 2006. Canada and Mexico together accounted for more than one-quarter of U.S. merchandise exports from small and medium-size companies.

New Records

While NAFTA critics say that the agreement has harmed U.S. manufacturing, U.S. industrial production—three-quarters of which is manufacturing—rose by 57% between 1993 and 2007.

This performance significantly outpaced the 28% increase in U.S. industrial production between 1981 and 1993.

In recent years, U.S. manufacturers have set new records for output, revenues, profits, profit rates, and return on investment prior to the recent financial crisis. At the same time, growth in America's service sectors—which employ some 80% of U.S. workers—has reduced the share of U.S. GDP represented by manufacturing from 15.6% in 1993 to about 12% in 2007.

However, U.S. manufacturers shed about three million jobs between 2000 and 2003, despite the dramatic growth in output since NAFTA entered into force. Where have the lost manufacturing jobs gone? Not to Canada or Mexico, nor to China or India. Rather, they've been lost to a country called "productivity."

A productivity revolution has allowed manufacturers to greatly increase output with fewer workers. Technological change, automation, and widespread use of information technologies have allowed firms to boost output even as some have cut payrolls.

This productivity revolution is a complex phenomenon. NAFTA critics are correct when they say that manufacturing employment hit a peak and then began a steady decline. However, the peak was in 1979, 15 years before NAFTA came into force.

Today, with American manufacturers facing severe difficulties in the face of a sharp recession, revenue from exports to Canada and Mexico is critical. More than 13 million Americans are employed in manufacturing. These workers produced $870 billion worth of exports in 2007. Canadians and Mexicans alone purchased $330 billion of U.S. manufactured goods in 2007.

In other words, the NAFTA market brings export revenue of $25,000 for each and every American factory worker. Compare this to the salary of the average U.S. manufacturing worker—about $37,000. How could manufacturers make their payroll without the revenues they earn by exporting to Canada and Mexico? The short answer is, they couldn't.

Agricultural Export Markets

For U.S. agriculture, NAFTA has been critical to export growth. Canada and Mexico account for 37% of the total increase in U.S. agricultural exports since 1993. Moreover, the share of total U.S. agricultural exports destined for Canada or Mexico has grown from 22% in 1993 to 30% in 2007.

Thanks in large part to NAFTA, Canada today is the top U.S. export destination for wheat, poultry, oats, eggs and potato exports. It is the second-largest U.S. export market for beef, pork, apples and soybean meal, and third largest for rice and dry edible bean exports.

NAFTA did even more to open the Mexican market for U.S. farmers and ranchers. Mexico's "MFN tariffs"—those paid by exporters from countries that lack a free trade agreement with Mexico—were highest for agricultural products; NAFTA allowed American farmers and ranchers to get past those barriers.

Thanks to this access, Mexico is the top U.S. export destination for beef, rice, soybean meal, apples, cheese and dry edible bean exports. It is the second-largest U.S. export market for corn, soybeans and oil, and third largest for pork, poultry, eggs, and cotton.

NAFTA is more important than ever. The members of the U.S. Chamber of Commerce have seen its benefits firsthand as it has generated new opportunities for workers, farmers, consumers and businesses. . . . NAFTA should continue to play the foundational role it has for the past 15 years.

> "Rather than encouraging sustainable and equitable growth, NAFTA has contributed to the loss of jobs and incomes of workers, while enriching the very few."

NAFTA Harms America

Thea M. Lee

Thea M. Lee is the policy director at the American Federation of Labor–Congress of Industrial Organizations (AFL-CIO). She was a former editor of Dollars & Sense *magazine and the author of* A Field Guide to the Global Economy. *In the following viewpoint, Lee represents the AFL-CIO before the U.S. Congress in claiming that the North American Free Trade Agreement (NAFTA) is failing workers in Canada, Mexico, and the United States. While the agreement does reward corporations, Lee states, it shows little regard for workers' wages or job security. As Lee maintains, half a million U.S. jobs have been lost due to NAFTA. In addition, the agreement gives corporations the power to influence governments and does not allow citizens or lawmakers a say in how NAFTA policies are carried out. For these reasons, she suggests that the NAFTA model be abandoned when negotiating future international trade agreements.*

Thea M. Lee, "Senate Testimony on NAFTA at Year 12," AFL-CIO, September 11, 2006. Reproduced by permission.

As you read, consider the following questions:

1. According to Lee, what was the combined trade deficit with Mexico and Canada in 2006, twelve years after NAFTA went into effect?

2. How does NAFTA undermine U.S. laws, in the author's view?

3. By how much has the U.S. trade surplus in services fallen between 1997 and 2005, according to Lee?

The North American Free Trade Agreement (NAFTA) was sold to the American public and American workers as a market-opening agreement that would create high-paying export-related jobs here in the United States, bring prosperity to Mexico, and spur economic growth and political stability throughout North America. The outcome has been quite different.

While it is true that trade and investment flows between the three North American countries have grown rapidly since NAFTA was implemented in 1994, on measures of much more importance to the average North American citizen, NAFTA has been a dismal failure. Workers in all three NAFTA countries have seen their wages fall or stagnate (failing to keep pace with productivity increases), as job insecurity and inequality have grown. At the same time, NAFTA rules have disadvantaged North American family farmers, many small businesses, consumers, and the environment relative to multinational corporate interests.

Rather than encouraging sustainable and equitable growth, NAFTA has contributed to the loss of jobs and incomes of workers, while enriching the very few. NAFTA's main outcome has been to strengthen the clout and bargaining power of multinational corporations, to limit the scope of governments to regulate in the public interest, and to force workers into more direct competition with each other, while assuring them fewer rights and protections. The increased capital mobility afforded by NAFTA has hurt workers, the environment, and communities in all three NAFTA countries.

The Loss of American Jobs

Advocates of NAFTA promised better access to a market of 90 million consumers on our southern border and prosperity for Mexico, yielding a "win-win" outcome. Yet [in 2006] more than twelve years after NAFTA went into effect, our combined trade deficit with Mexico and Canada has ballooned from $9 billion to $127 billion. The Labor Department has certified that well over half a million U.S. workers lost their jobs due to NAFTA (through 2002, when the NAFTA-TAA [Transitional Adjustment Assistance] program was merged with other trade-displacement programs), while the Economic Policy Institute estimates that the ballooning NAFTA trade deficit contributed to the loss of more than one million jobs and job opportunities.

Even workers who have kept their jobs have seen wages, benefits, and bargaining power eroded under NAFTA. Professor Kate Bronfenbrenner at Cornell University found that since NAFTA was put in place, employers have increasingly used the threat of shifting production to stifle union organizing drives or to block first contracts.

No Benefits for Mexico

One of the main advantages of NAFTA was supposed to be that it would alleviate poverty and low wages in Mexico, helping bring the U.S. and Mexico closer together. However, on this front also, it has fallen short. Real wages in Mexico are actually lower today than before NAFTA was put in place, and the number of people in poverty grew from 62 million to 69 million (through 2003). The number of people crossing the border illegally is estimated to have doubled, contrary to predictions of NAFTA boosters, including then-President [Carlos] Salinas.

Furthermore, Mexico now faces difficult transitions in its farm sector, as the last round of NAFTA's agricultural tariffs are phased out. And the rapid maquiladora [factory that imports materials duty free and then exports products made from them back to the provider nation] employment growth of the 1990s is fading fast, as multinational corporations shift more production to China and other low-wage locations, where workers' rights are severely repressed. These are the logical consequences of a free trade agreement that relied solely on lowering trade barriers and protecting corporate interests, but failed to build an adequate social dimension.

Corporate Power over Governments

NAFTA undermines our laws by allowing corporations to sue governments and challenge statutes protecting the environment, public health and consumers. In some cases, corporations have even collected compensation from governments for lost profits or other damages. Legislators and ordinary citizens have no effective voice in the dispute resolution process, even though it is the laws they have voted for that are under attack.

NAFTA restricts the ability of governments to regulate services delivered across borders and by foreign investors. Under NAFTA, we have had to open the border to Mexican trucks even though we cannot ensure that each of these trucks meets our health and safety standards. Public services have been threatened as well—a case against Canada's postal service under NAFTA is still under way, and has disturbing implications for our governments' ability to regulate and support other essential public services.

NAFTA doesn't allow governments in Canada, Mexico and the U.S. to include local preferences or workers' rights criteria in making purchasing decisions. In fact, when President [Bill] Clinton issued an executive order banning the federal procurement of goods made with the worst forms of child labor in 1999, he had to exclude Canada and Mexico from the or-

North American Views on NAFTA

*Thinking about the North American Free Trade Agreement
(or NAFTA) that includes Canada, the United States, and Mexico,
what effect has NAFTA had on the U.S. economy? Has it been...?*

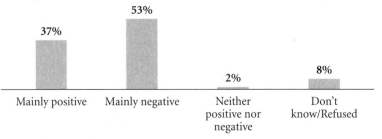

Canadian Views on NAFTA

*Thinking about the North American Free Trade Agreement
(or NAFTA) that includes Canada, the United States, and Mexico,
what effect has NAFTA had on Canada's economy? Has it been...?*

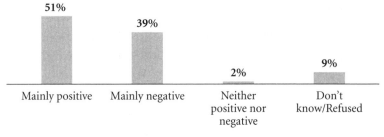

Mexican Views on NAFTA

*Thinking about the North American Free Trade Agreement
(or NAFTA) that includes Canada, the United States, and Mexico,
what effect has NAFTA had on Mexico's economy? Has it been...?*

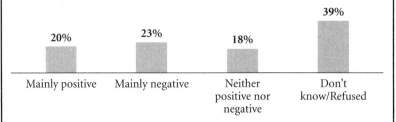

TAKEN FROM: Cynthia English, "Opinion Briefing: North American
Free Trade Agreement." Gallup, December 12, 2008.

der, because banning goods made by child slave labor would have violated NAFTA's government procurement provisions.

Finally, the NAFTA labor side agreement has utterly failed to protect workers' rights. None of the 34 cases filed under the side agreement has progressed beyond the initial stage of co-operative consultations, and no labor rights violators have faced any penalties under the accord. No government has paid a penny in fines, and no trade sanctions have been imposed (or even threatened). A UCLA [University of California at Los Angeles] study of the labor side agreement found that its in-herent weaknesses, and a lack of political will among the par-ties to implement it aggressively, may doom the accord to "oblivion."

Citizens and Lawmakers Excluded

On March 23, 2005, in Waco, Texas, the presidents of the United States, Mexico and Canada launched a new initiative, the Security and Prosperity Partnership for North America (SPP), to "increase security and enhance prosperity . . . through greater cooperation and information sharing." While the twin goals of greater security and prosperity are ones we support, we have deep reservations about the processes set out to reach them in this instance. It appears that important deci-sions related to deepening economic integration among our three nations, and the well-being of our citizens, are being made by government and business elites, while civil society and Congress are sidelined.

In 2005, each nation established "Prosperity Working Groups" to consider and carry out proposals on a number of issues, including: manufactured goods and sectoral and re-gional competitiveness; movement of goods; energy; environ-ment; e-commerce and information communications tech-nologies; financial services; business facilitation; food and agriculture; transportation; and health. These working groups are supposed to consult with "stakeholders" in undertaking their activities. However, it appears that for the U.S. working groups, consultation outside of business circles has been minimal at best. The working group on manufactured goods, for example, is contemplating the integration of the auto and steel sectors of North America. There is little indication to date, however, that unions in these sectors will have any substantial input as to how such integration should be deepened.

Further evidence of the corporate domination of this process was the formation of the North American Competitiveness Council (NACC) in March 2006. The NACC was formed to discuss ways to enhance competitiveness through further elimination of regulations and other barriers to trade. The non-governmental representatives invited to participate in this council include Campbell Soup Co., Chevron, Ford, FedEx, General Electric, General Motors, Kansas City Southern Industries, Lockheed Martin Corp., Merck, Mittal Steel USA, New York Life, United Parcel Service, Wal-Mart and Whirlpool.

In order for the SPP to be mutually beneficial to average citizens in North America, civil society must have the ability to participate meaningfully in these discussions. Simply submitting comments through the SPP website is not enough. Before the SPP process goes further, the task forces and councils advising our government must be expanded beyond business circles.

NAFTA in Context

One often-cited argument for NAFTA was that it would improve U.S. competitiveness with the rest of the world. However, since NAFTA was put in place, our overall trade deficit has also ballooned, from $75 billion in 1993 to $726 billion in 2005. The current account deficit hit a dangerously high 6 percent of GDP [gross domestic product] at the end of 2005, slowing any possibility of strong economic recovery and undermining the potential for future job growth. The high import propensity of the U.S. economy means that even as economic recovery gets under way, a large proportion of every dollar spent by consumers goes to purchase imports, undermining the economy's ability to generate good jobs at home.

These figures are very real to working Americans who are losing family-supporting jobs and benefits as manufacturing and even service jobs are lost overseas.

[The 2006] trade figures reveal other startling weaknesses in the U.S. economy, even in those areas which have traditionally been considered U.S. strongholds, like services and advanced technology products. The trade surplus in services has fallen from $92 billion in 1997 to $56 billion in 2005. In advanced technology products, similarly, the U.S. surplus of $4.5 billion in 2001 had turned into a whopping deficit of $44 billion by 2005, most of that with China. The long-time U.S. trade surplus in agriculture has pretty much evaporated, including in products that compete with U.S. goods. These trends call into question the conventional wisdom that the United States enjoys a permanent and growing comparative advantage in the export of services, high-technology goods, and agriculture.

In general, the experience of our unions and our members with past trade agreements has led us to question critically the extravagant claims often made on their behalf. While these agreements are inevitably touted as market-opening agreements that will significantly expand U.S. export opportunities (and therefore create export-related U.S. jobs), the impact has more often been to facilitate the shift of U.S. investment offshore. In fact, the agreements' far-reaching protections for foreign investors directly facilitate the shift of investment, and such shifts can fairly be considered an integral goal of these so-called "trade" agreements. Much, although not all, of this investment has gone into production for export back to the United States, boosting U.S. imports and displacing rather than creating U.S. jobs.

The net impact has been a negative swing in our trade balance with most of the countries with which we have negotiated free trade agreements. While we understand that many other factors influence bilateral trade balances (including most notably growth trends and exchange rate movements), it is nonetheless striking that most of our FTAs [free trade agreements] have yielded worsening trade balances. Moreover, our overall trade balance has continued to deteriorate rapidly, even as we pursue an aggressive FTA strategy.

If the goal of these so-called "free trade" agreements is truly to improve U.S. competitiveness and open foreign markets to American exports (and not to reward and encourage companies that shift more jobs overseas), it is pretty clear the strategy is not working. Before Congress approves new bilateral free trade agreements based on the outdated NAFTA model, it is imperative that we take some time to figure out how and why the current policy has failed.

Free Trade or Fair Trade?

The AFL-CIO believes that increased international trade and investment can yield broad and substantial benefits, both to American working families, and to our brothers and sisters around the world—if done right. Trade agreements must include enforceable protections for core workers' rights and must preserve our ability to use our domestic trade laws effectively. They must protect our government's ability to regulate in the public interest, to use procurement dollars to promote economic development and other legitimate social goals, and to provide high quality public services. Finally, it is essential that workers, their unions, and other civil society organizations be able to participate meaningfully in our government's trade policy process, on an equal footing with corporate interests.

NAFTA is a model that has utterly failed to deliver the promised benefits to ordinary citizens in any of the three

North American countries. Yet our government is in the process of negotiating new trade agreements with dozens of countries, using NAFTA as a template.

The success or failure of any future trade and investment agreements will hinge on governments' willingness and ability to negotiate agreements that appropriately address all of the social, economic, and political dimensions of trade and investment, not just those of concern to corporations. Unfortunately, NAFTA is precisely the wrong starting point.

"The benefits to the U.S. economy are obvious: prices move lower for consumers and profits rise for corporations."

Outsourcing Benefits America

Victor A. Canto

In the following viewpoint, Victor A. Canto, a contributing editor to the National Review Online, claims that contrary to the general public opinion, outsourcing benefits America instead of causing economic decline. Canto contends that outsourcing jobs actually reduces costs for consumers and causes a rise in profits for corporations. He also argues that outsourcing jobs offshore benefits other nations, creating a win-win situation.

As you read, consider the following questions:

1. According to Canto, what might the restriction of outsourcing by U.S. companies do?

2. What effect does the outsourcing of payroll departments and software operations have on American workers?

3. According to the viewpoint, "while it is easier to get laid off in America than in Europe it is also easier to find a job in America." What is the result of this?

Victor A. Canto, "Outsourcing Is the American Way: In Spite of What Pundits Say, the U.S. Wins When Jobs Go Offshore," *National Review Online*, April 6, 2004. http://www.nationalreview.com/nrof_canto/canto200404060834.asp.

U.S. manufacturing jobs have been going abroad for de-cades. Now, however, workers in a wide range of other fields—from accounting to electrical engineering—are discovering that their jobs aren't immune from offshore outsourcing. For the past decade American companies have shipped computer programming and call-center jobs to India, the Philippines, Mexico, Canada, and other places where educated workers reside. Economists maintain that globalization benefits the U.S. as old-economy jobs that move abroad are replaced by better, higher-value jobs at home. Yet many Americans don't buy it. Polls show that anxiety over job security is a top voter concern.

America Benefits from Outsourcing

In spite of what is said in much of the press, the greatest beneficiary of outsourcing is the U.S. itself. We import many more jobs than we export. Foreign companies all over the world are attracted by our political stability and high worker productivity. Efforts to restrict outsourcing by U.S. companies may backfire, especially if they provoke retaliation by U.S. trading partners.

Contrary to the statements of many politicians, the outsourcing phenomenon is easily understood in the context of traditional economic analysis. The calculus—outsourcing situation by outsourcing situation—is fairly straightforward. Look at two of the main outsourcing culprits.

Mexico. The origins of outsourcing here can be traced to NAFTA, signed in 1993. The elimination of trade barriers created profit opportunities for the production of goods and services in Mexico. Even though productivity was lower in Mexico than in the U.S., and there were additional transportation costs, the wages in the country were low enough to compensate. The search for higher profits led to a shift in production facilities to Mexico. U.S. consumers were happy because they were able to buy similar products at lower prices. Mexican workers were happy as the higher demand for labor services resulted in higher wages. The standard of living for Mexican workers rose. NAFTA was a win-win situation.

India. Over the last decade, India and the Asian tigers (and China later on) embarked on market-oriented economic policies. But technology has added a different twist to India's outsourcing story. The capacity of fiber-optic lines that connect telephone systems into India increased almost sevenfold in 2001 and 2002. Increased bandwidth, falling prices, compression, and secure methods of connectivity reduced the "transportation costs" of sending work India's way. Information-based jobs are especially vulnerable because it is easy and cheap to transmit data almost anywhere these days. That's exactly what happened in India's case. So-called "placeless jobs"—animation, application and insurance-claims processing, benefit administration, desktop publishing, digitizing, financial analysis for Wall Street banks, accounting and bookkeeping, tax preparation, medical transcription and billings, telemarketing—jobs that don't require face-to-face customer interaction, have gone to India (and other wired-in regions).

Benefits to The U.S. and Other Nations

The benefits to the U.S. economy are obvious: prices move lower for consumers and profits rise for corporations. As for U.S. workers displaced by outsourcing, they are—once displaced—able to move to other more-productive, higher value-added activities.

The benefits to India are also evident. India's National Association of Software and Service Companies estimates that more than 300,000 white-collar jobs serving overseas clients have been created in the country since 2000. But more importantly the salaries of the most sought-after workers are surging, offsetting the cost savings that lure U.S. companies overseas. In other words, outsourcing is also raising the standard of living of foreign workers.

High-Paying Jobs Stay Here

American companies generally outsource work to India or China that requires little skill or training. The high-end work and wages stay here; but in fact, they might not be retained if the stateside work were not augmented by outsourced functions in lower-cost countries. Furthermore, workers freed up from routine tasks that have been outsourced are often redeployed within the company to higher-paying jobs, or on projects that generate greater value-added services or products.

Bruce Bartlett,
National Center for Policy Analysis, July 27, 2004.

Executives are also developing a keen sense of how critical it is to keep core managers—people who know the product and how customers use it—in the United States. Core development for new products remains in the U.S. where engineers are closer to marketing teams. In other words, the high value-added jobs still remain here and afford opportunities for displaced workers with the necessary skills.

Outsourcing, coupled with the explosion of global trade, has also transformed delivery into a complex engineering task. Contrary to popular belief, the U.S. is creating new high-paying jobs, and logistics is one of the latest growing fields. Yes, we allow companies to freely outsource their payroll departments and software operations. But that frees American workers to concentrate on new cutting-edge (i.e., higher value-added) activities like logistics.

Outsourcing Is a Political Issue

It's not hard to see why outsourcing has become such a major political issue. The benefits of outsourcing—lower prices and higher profits—are spread out among shareholders and consumers. Consumers see lower prices and shareholders see higher profits. The stock market, when strong enough, offsets any protectionist pressure generated by the fear of job losses due to higher imports or job outsourcing. The investor class understands that a rising tide lifts all boats.

In contrast, the costs of outsourcing are concentrated in a particular special-interest group—displaced employees. And this group is supported by many powerful political voices.

An example is the tension mounting within the National Association of Manufacturers, with many smaller members urging the big lobbying group to do more to fight the migration of jobs overseas—even as many of the larger members embrace the trend. The larger companies are more likely to have multi-plant facilities all over the world and thus may be the ones taking advantage of outsourcing. But the smaller companies are likely to be the single-plant facilities that are threatened by the outsourcing drive.

In another example, the AFL-CIO has filed an unprecedented petition against China under Section 301 of the 1974 Trade Act. It alleges that China's "brutal repression" of workers' rights gives its manufacturing sector a cost savings between 10 percent and 77 percent and has led to a loss of 727,000 American jobs.

Proposed Legislation and the Result of Outsourcing

It's not surprising that politicians catering to the union vote are likely to be the sponsors of protectionist legislation. (When the Bush administration gave into steel protectionism, it was a deliberate attempt to buy some of the union vote in the steel-producing states. It did not work and luckily the administration gave up on the protectionist slant.) Dozens of bills to protect U.S. jobs have been introduced in state legislatures and Congress. Some bills would require state contract work be done in the U.S. Other proposed legislation would require workers at call centers to disclose their location to consumers. Finally, there are bills that would restrict companies from bringing foreign workers to the U.S. on guest visas to do jobs previously done by Americans. This is an ironic piece of legislation; employees not allowed by the U.S. to immigrate permanently come here for a period, get training, and then go back and work in outsourced industries.

Some Americans will accept less prosperity and opportunity in return for more stability and security (unions do that), but the trend is not going that way. It the private sector the majority would choose prosperity and opportunity. While it is easier to get laid off in America than in Europe it is also easier to find a job in America. The result is a constantly rejuvenating economy. Take the former rust belt where the complaints about outsourcing are the loudest. Data shows that Ohio has imported 242,000 jobs, Indiana 163,000, and Michigan 244,000. Outsourcing isn't a symptom of America's decline. It is part of a process that prevents decline.

| "What is good for companies' bottom lines may not necessarily be good for America.

Outsourcing Harms America

Ronil Hira

In the following viewpoint, Ronil Hira argues that America is losing its competitive edge by outsourcing jobs to foreign markets. According to Hira, many U.S. workers—including high-tech workers—are being displaced by outsourcing, and not nearly enough are finding new positions quickly. Hira also contends that the new jobs promised to these displaced workers are not typically better-paying or more secure than the jobs they lost to outsourcing. Hira is an assistant professor of public policy at the Rochester Institute of Technology in New York and a senior member of the Institute of Electrical and Electronics Engineers.

As you read, consider the following questions:

1. As Hira relates, of the 65 percent of displaced employees in 2004 who found new work, what percent earned as much money as they had at their previous jobs?

Ronil Hira, Testimony to the U.S.-China Economic Security Review Commission on Offshoring of Software and High Technology Jobs, January 13, 2005.

2. What evidence does the author provide to support his claim that high-level engineering jobs are being moved offshore?

3. In Hira's view, why is it difficult to identify workers who have been displaced by outsourcing?

Many economists believe that the amount of offshoring has little or no effect on the overall number of US jobs and the unemployment rate, at least in the medium run. They use a full employment model, so they assume that the US labor market clears eventually. However, most economists agree that offshoring causes the following: 1) job displacement for US workers; 2) a change in the mix of US occupations; and, 3) wage pressure for US jobs that are now tradable across borders.

There is little disagreement that some US workers will lose their jobs as their work shifts overseas. The *hope* is that displaced workers will be reemployed rapidly and at substantially the same wages. It appears that this process, sometimes called 'adjustment', is not happening rapidly, or not at all, for thousands of displaced technology workers. The reason seems to be the unusually low levels of job creation in the economy over the past few years. Many have called our most recent recovery from recession, a job-less one. Unfortunately, there are few good explanations for why the recovery has not generated the number of jobs we would expect. Some have said that it is due to productivity increases, but that explanation is simply a tautology.

The latest Bureau of Labor Statistics' Displaced Worker Survey, released in January 2004, provides us some insight into the reemployment rates for workers. For workers who were displaced between 2001–2003, it shows that 35% were unemployed in January 2004, and of the 65% who were employed, only 43% earned at least as much as they did before displacement. So, the empirical data do not support the economists' hope that displaced workers will be reemployed rapidly and at substantially the same wages.

These results are mostly consistent with longer term results from the displaced worker surveys conducted from 1979 onwards. A large share of displaced workers remain unemployed for extended periods of time, and even for those lucky enough to find work many take substantial pay cuts.

Better Jobs Not Guaranteed

The second effect that economists predict is offshoring will cause a change in the mix of US occupations as some jobs migrate to more efficient (i.e., lower cost labor) locations. As the US loses its engineering and other high skill jobs to more efficient locations, Americans will simply move into other occupations. However, there is no guarantee that the new blend of US occupations will be better after offshoring. In fact, no economist is able to explain the types of new jobs that will be created. Most, including [then] Federal Reserve Chairman Alan Greenspan, have only given vague answers about the jobs of the future needing higher skills. If we relinquish our engineering and computer programming jobs, will we be able to replace them with better jobs? This is a key policy question that no one can answer.

It is also a very practical question that I get asked at nearly every IEEE [Institute of Electrical and Electronics Engineers] meeting I attend. Invariably, someone asks, "What new job should I be training for? What skill sets do I need?" Unfortunately, I have no good answer for them, and I have yet to find a good one from anyone else.

The third predicted effect is wage depression in jobs that are now tradable across borders. As I mentioned earlier, these are already apparent in the IEEE-USA latest surveys.

All of these effects, plus the lack of reliable data, are understandably creating a high degree of insecurity amongst US technology workers. . . .

High-Skill Jobs Going Overseas

Some have argued that only low level jobs are moving overseas. As one major news magazine put it, why should the US be concerned if 'mind-numbing' computer coding moves offshore. They argue that it simply frees up American workers to do more interesting tasks. This may comfort some, but the empirical evidence does not support the notion that only low level tasks are moving offshore.

It is clear that high-level engineering design has begun to move offshore. Many top technology firms, such as Microsoft, Intel, Google and others, have created research and development centers in low-cost countries. Venture capital firms, what some consider the lifeblood of future innovation, are increasingly asking the firms they fund to offshore as much as possible. I participated on the keynote plenary panel discussion in Silicon Valley at [the 2004] IEEE Hot Chips conference, a conference that brings together designers of the most advanced integrated circuits. Offshoring is an important enough issue even for the most advanced electronics designers to have it as a special event at their annual conference. On the panel with me were two venture capitalists, Carl Everett from Accel Partners and Vinod Dham from NewPath Ventures, both of whom said that they were pressing the start-up firms they fund, firms that design advanced electronics, to offshore as much work as possible. Another method for assessing the types of jobs moving offshore is by searching the job openings posted on the websites of major technology corporations such as Intel and Oracle. It shows a number of high level engineering openings at their Chinese operations. Many of these openings require advanced degrees and experience.

We are also seeing high-level non-engineering support functions move offshore. Professors Martin Kenney and Rafiq Dossani completed a revealing case study of a major US high-technology firm. The firm began to move some of its financial operations to its office in Bangalore [India] in 2001, and it

A Broad and Deep Impact

Each time we transfer knowledge bases overseas, whether it be manufacturing or technology or research, that is a service that will obviously be performed by a competing economy—whether emerging or not, a competing economy. And it is work that will not be done by the U.S. economy and our workers. The result is—and this is at the margins at this point, but could grow to an increasingly larger share of the trade-deficit problem—the result is further pressure on the U.S. economy.

And a further impact in terms of labor is not just the loss of jobs. Study after study, survey after survey, shows that every job that replaces one that is outsourced pays approximately 20 percent less than the job that was exported overseas. So we have a continuing downward pressure on wages in this country. That has an impact on education because obviously that money's not available to the tax base that pays for education. It diminishes, in point of fact, the income-tax base for the federal government and state governments. So the impact is broad and it is deep.

Lou Dobbs,
Mother Jones, *February 7, 2005.*

was so successful that they eventually made the office the headquarters for many finance functions serving the company's offices around the world. Many of these functions require the highest skill levels. In their study, Kenney and Dossani found that moving the function to Bangalore reduced costs, reduced headcount and improved quality. Plus, they found that the company was able to ramp up the offshore process much more rapidly than they had even planned.

There is no doubt that there will be failures along the way, but it is clear that the overwhelming trend is for work to move offshore. . . .

Compensating Displaced Workers

By offshoring, company executives are pursuing what they believe is in the best interest of their shareholders. They believe that offshoring will improve their profits by cutting costs.

They should not be vilified for doing offshoring, since it is what they are expected to do. On the other hand, workers too are acting rationally by voicing their concerns about how offshoring will affect their livelihoods.

But as I said earlier, even mainstream economists agree that offshoring does not guarantee that the US will be better off. What is good for companies' bottom lines may not necessarily be good for America. We should be focused on designing policies that ensure the very best outcome for America.

Unfortunately, the offshore outsourcing of high-skill jobs has a number of characteristics that make it hard to compensate those who are adversely affected:

1. It is often difficult to directly identify workers who have been displaced, many of whom may not even know that they have been displaced because of trade. Companies are increasingly reluctant to reveal their plans for fear of the bad publicity that will result. Many workers are too intimidated to publicly identify themselves. They fear losing the severance package offered by their employers or that they will be blacklisted if they speak out.

2. Even if we could identify those who have been adversely affected by trade, it is not clear how we should compensate them. Do we offer subsidized re-training in some other profession?

3. Re-training and other types of assistance programs are very difficult to implement. Is it realistic to expect an electrical engineer with 20 years of experience to spend four years studying to become a nurse?

In sum, we think it is entirely misleading to describe off-shore outsourcing as a "Win-Win" proposition for America and other countries, as free trade advocates so often do. The burden should be placed on those advocates to demonstrate how workers who have been adversely affected will be compensated and helped to become productive citizens once again.

These advocates assume, as part of their argument, that displaced American workers will be re-deployed. Instead of assuming, we should ensure that such workers are redeployed in equally high skill and highly paid positions.

> *"We can start [a U.S. economic recovery] today by 'Buying American—Building American—Being American!'"*

"Buy American" Policies Benefit America

Jaime Maliszewski

Jaime Maliszewski is the president of a metal plating and finishing business in Milwaukee, Wisconsin. In the following viewpoint, Maliszewski argues that America's demand for cheaper products has prompted companies to outsource to foreign markets. But this strategy, he claims, has ultimately cost American jobs and has failed to make the country stronger. Maliszewski insists that the United States must recover these lost jobs and focus on creating incentives to purchase American products. In his view, Americans owe it to their country to "buy American" so that the nation—as a whole—can overcome its current financial crisis.

As you read, consider the following questions:

1. Why does Maliszewski think an economic "bail out" is not what America needs?

Jaime Maliszewski, "Buy American! Be American!" BizTimes.com, February 26, 2009. Reproduced by permission.

2. Why does the author believe that the American public shares the blame for sending jobs overseas?

3. What problems does Maliszewski blame on buying foreign goods?

John F. Kennedy had it right [in 1961] when he told Americans, "Ask not what your country can do for you, but what you can do for your country!"

We have forgotten this rallying cry and have gotten lazy, causing this current [economic] mess we are now so desperate to fix. We became dependent on our government for everything and now we all want to be "bailed out."

This won't work! It will only postpone the inevitable, unless we *all* decide to roll up our sleeves and work our way out of it.

Perils of Buying Cheap

We need to bring work and jobs back into this country so that we have people/consumers with money that can buy our products. Sending all of our manufacturing jobs to foreign countries took our best-paying jobs with them, leaving too few consumers behind with jobs to buy our goods.

I know it is easy to blame big business for sending these jobs to foreign countries, but the American buying public is just as much to blame. We buy cheap, without any care for where or how an item is made.

How can you blame big business for trying to make cheaper products when that is what we are demanding? Granted, big business took the easy way out and sent the work over rather then finding better/leaner ways to operate, but then again, many of the unions fought this progress, cutting their own throats.

Big business had it half right in the 1980s when they marketed "Buy American." It should have included "Build American," because in the 1990s they started buying many of their

The Buy American Act

Some argue that the Buy American Act has outlived its usefulness in today's global economy. I argue that it is as relevant today as it was when it was enacted in 1933. The passage of seventy years has not diminished the importance of this act for American manufacturing companies or for those who are employed in this crucial sector of our economy. In fact, a strong argument can be made that this act is even more necessary today than it was seventy years ago. With American jobs heading overseas at an alarming rate, the government should be doing all it can to make sure that U.S. taxpayer dollars are spent to support American jobs.

Some argue that the Buy American Act is protectionist and anti–free trade. I disagree. Supporting American industry is not protectionist—it is common sense. The erosion of our manufacturing base needs to be stopped, and Congress should support procurement and trade policies that help to ensure that we do not continue to lose portions of this vital segment of our economy.

Russ Feingold, speech to U.S. Senate, July 29, 2003.

manufactured goods from foreign countries or even opened American companies overseas or in Mexico.

Take Wal-Mart, for example. When Sam Walton started the company, he proudly marketed "Buy American." Now, you would be hard-pressed to find American-made products in his stores.

Better example, look what buying foreign goods has gotten us. Poisoned pet food and toothpaste, as well as toys with lead paint with little or no safety standards. Child labor abuse has skyrocketed worldwide and world pollution levels have increased due to the non-regulation or non-enforcement of pollution laws in the countries that build these products. Worker safety and care are also non-existent in many of these countries, as well.

Take Care of America First

Sending jobs to foreign countries to lower our costs does not and did not work. It did not work in our free market system because it eliminated the buying power (jobs) of the people who make up our market, our consumers.

It *is* that simple.

All businesses outsource work, either to lower costs because someone else has a better way of making the product or because they need to increase their capacity. My brothers and I do this in our three companies (but only with American companies). However, now that times are tough and sales are down, we have brought many of these jobs back into our shops to better utilize our people and assets.

We are working harder, smarter and for less money just to survive these tough times. We know we need to take care of our own first. We also buy all of our equipment from American companies, even all of our company and personal cars are American-made. We, as a country, need to pull the outsourced work back into this country. We don't need cash bail outs, we need work.

Building roads and schools is good, but stimulus payments back to the American people are only a Band Aid. We need jobs, and to get jobs, we need to bring the work back.

Create incentives to buy American. Eliminate all the pet projects of our congressmen and women from the stimulus bill and work on helping to bring work back into this country. Hard work built this country, and hard work will save it!

As Americans we need to take back our country and have pride and loyalty in being the best country in the world. Stop blaming the other side and start doing what you can for your country. We don't need to wait for the stimulus. We can start today by "Buying American—Building American—Being American!" This goes for every American citizen, whether you are buying for your company or your family!

| "The 'Buy American' provisions are dangerous protectionist policies thinly guised as feel-good patriotism."

"Buy American" Policies Harm America

Gary Shapiro

In the viewpoint that follows, Gary Shapiro, the president and CEO of the Consumer Electronics Association, states that "Buy American" policies will not help the United States get out of its current financial crisis. Shapiro contends that encouraging Americans to buy only American goods may prompt foreign countries to enact equally protectionist policies and thus damage U.S. trade opportunities overseas. He insists that the losses from such retaliatory measures would only worsen America's economic situation.

As you read, consider the following questions:

1. According to the Peterson Institute, as cited by the author, how many U.S. jobs could be lost if other countries adopted protectionist strategies in response to a U.S. "Buy American" policy?

Gary Shapiro, "'Buy American' Sounds Patriotic, but the Protectionist Policy Could Start a Trade War," Huffington Post, February 16, 2009. Reproduced by permission.

2. Between 1993 and 2006, how many U.S. jobs were created due to America's global leadership, as Shapiro reports?

3. As Shapiro claims, what U.S. tariff act deepened the Depression in 1930?

The world cheered when President Barack Obama took the oath of office—many hopeful that this young leader would emerge as a guiding light for the global economic crisis and restore America's reputation as a wise and generous neighbor. President Obama warned that we are in the greatest financial crisis since the Great Depression and offered up a nearly $800 billion economic stimulus package to create jobs, support states and protect the country's future. At the same time, President Obama urged lawmakers combing through proposed investments that "we can't send a protectionist message."

What happened?

Tucked inside the nearly 700-page stimulus text is a short clause that sounds at face value as cheerful as vanilla ice cream on warm apple pie. It's called "Buy American" and it provides that all iron, steel and manufactured goods used in stimulus-funded projects be produced in America. As Senator Sherrod Brown, a Democrat from Ohio, put it to the *New York Times*: "Who could be against it? Well, some Ivy League economists don't like it—something about Smoot-Hawley and the Great Depression."

The Protectionist Threat

Perhaps too much time has passed since the financial crisis of the 1930s or our lawmakers are not reading their history books. The "Buy American" provisions are dangerous protectionist policies thinly guised as feel-good patriotism. Politicians know that with American jobs being lost they must be seen as doing something to put people back to work. But history teaches us that policies designed to prop up a country's economy and its industries tend to backfire. Countries rush to save themselves, stop trading with one another, and endanger the global system.

The "Buy American" provisions will signal to our trading partners around the world that the United States is returning to the bad old days of protectionism and economic nationalism. Rather than stimulate the American economy, these provisions will lead to retaliation from abroad and cost precious jobs in the United States.

The Peterson Institute for International Economics, a nonpartisan think tank, estimated that a few thousand jobs would be created by "Buy American" whereas as many as 65,000 jobs could be lost if other countries put similar laws in place.

The United States' global economic leadership is not a guaranteed thing. It is something we build and maintain every day with our ideas, our products and our longstanding policy of international engagement. That leadership has paid huge dividends for Americans, contributing to an increase of 25 million jobs in the United States between 1993 and 2006—a period that coincided with an unprecedented expansion of U.S. trade policy.

Limiting Trade Opportunities

"Buy American" is poised to unravel much of that trade policy, putting at risk previous trade agreements and violating other concessions made to our trading partners. That lawmakers say that the provisions are consistent with the letter of World Trade Organization rules is meaningless if the effect of "Buy American" is to turn our country inward and halt trading opportunities.

If we reverse ourselves on trade now, the negative impact will be felt across the globe. We don't have to speculate about this. We know what happens when the United States makes a conscious step toward protectionism, ratcheting up tariffs and closing its borders to the outside world.

The Smoot-Hawley Tariff Act of 1930 helped precipitate a decade-long economic downturn. In our increasingly global economy, the effects of such a move today may well be even more disastrous. Both established markets like ours and fragile emerging markets in the developing world now depend on the free flow of goods and services. If we shut off that flow, we'll hurt ourselves, abandon the developing world and irreparably damage the global leadership we've fought so hard to establish.

Trade is not to blame for our economic crisis. Indeed, continuing our global leadership on trade may pave the clearest path back to prosperity, not just for our nation but for the world at large. Our new leaders in Congress and in the White House must reject the inevitable protectionist propaganda and do what they know to be right for our country.

"'Free trade' and 'globalization' are the guises behind which class war is being conducted against the middle class."

U.S. Free Trade Policy Is Fueling a Class War

Paul Craig Roberts

In the following viewpoint, Paul Craig Roberts claims that the outsourcing of American jobs to other nations is harming U.S. economic strength. According to Roberts, America is losing manufacturing jobs as well as professional positions because of rampant globalization. This job loss, he maintains, is eroding the nation's middle and working classes. Because he believes that the only job growth occurring in the United States is in low-skill service industries, Roberts argues that the country will experience a widening gap between a growing lower class and the very wealthy business owners. Roberts is an economist and syndicated columnist who served as assistant secretary of the Treasury under President Ronald Reagan.

As you read, consider the following questions:

1. According to Roberts, why did America once have no fear of cheap labor abroad?

Paul Craig Roberts, "As Jobs Leave America's Shores . . . The New Face of Class War," Counterpunch, September 30/October 1, 2006. Reproduced by permission.

2. As the author reports, how many manufacturing jobs were lost in the United States between 2001 and 2006?

3. Why does Roberts deem the growth in nontradable domestic service positions insignificant?

The attacks on middle-class jobs are lending new meaning to the phrase "class war." The ladders of upward mobility are being dismantled. America, the land of opportunity, is giving way to ever deepening polarization between rich and poor.

The assault on jobs predates the [George W.] Bush regime. However, the loss of middle-class jobs has become particularly intense in the 21st century, and, like other pressing problems, has been ignored by President Bush, who is focused on waging war in the Middle East and building a police state at home. The lives and careers that are being lost to the carnage of a gratuitous war in Iraq are paralleled by the economic destruction of careers, families, and communities in the U.S.A. Since the days of President Franklin D. Roosevelt in the 1930s, the U.S. government has sought to protect employment of its citizens. Bush has turned his back on this responsibility. He has given his support to the offshoring of American jobs that is eroding the living standards of Americans. It is another example of his betrayal of the public trust.

Outsourcing America

"Free trade" and "globalization" are the guises behind which class war is being conducted against the middle class by both political parties. Patrick J. Buchanan, a three-time contender for the presidential nomination, put it well when he wrote that NAFTA [North American Free Trade Agreement] and the various so-called trade agreements were never trade deals. The agreements were enabling acts that enabled U.S. corporations to dump their American workers, avoid Social Security taxes, health care and pensions, and move their factories offshore to locations where labor is cheap.

The offshore outsourcing of American jobs has nothing to do with free trade based on comparative advantage. Offshoring is labor arbitrage. First world capital and technology are not seeking comparative advantage at home in order to compete abroad. They are seeking absolute advantage abroad in cheap labor.

Two recent developments made possible the supremacy of absolute over comparative advantage: the high speed Internet and the collapse of world socialism, which opened China's and India's vast under-utilized labor resources to first world capital.

In times past, first world workers had nothing to fear from cheap labor abroad. Americans worked with superior capital, technology and business organization. This made Americans far more productive than Indians and Chinese, and, as it was not possible for U.S. firms to substitute cheaper foreign labor for U.S. labor, American jobs and living standards were not threatened by low wages abroad or by the products that these low wages produced.

The advent of offshoring has made it possible for U.S. firms using first world capital and technology to produce goods and services for the U.S. market with foreign labor. The result is to separate Americans' incomes from the production of the goods and services that they consume. This new development, often called "globalization," allows cheap foreign labor to work with the same capital, technology and business know-how as U.S. workers. The foreign workers are now as productive as Americans, with the difference being that the large excess supply of labor that overhangs labor markets in China and India keeps wages in these countries low. Labor that is equally productive but paid a fraction of the wage is a magnet for Western capital and technology.

Destroying Entire Industries

Although a new development, offshoring is destroying entire industries, occupations and communities in the United States.

The devastation of U.S. manufacturing employment was waved away with promises that a "new economy" based on high-tech knowledge jobs would take its place. Education and retraining were touted as the answer.

In testimony before the U.S.-China Commission, I explained that offshoring is the replacement of U.S. labor with foreign labor in U.S. production functions over a wide range of tradable goods and services. (Tradable goods and services are those that can be exported or that are competitive with imports. Nontradable goods and services are those that only have domestic markets and no import competition. For example, barbers and dentists offer nontradable services. Examples of nontradable goods are perishable, locally produced fruits and vegetables and specially fabricated parts of local machine shops.) As the production of most tradable goods and services can be moved offshore, there are no replacement occupations for which to train except in domestic "hands on" services such as barbers, manicurists, and hospital orderlies. No country benefits from trading its professional jobs, such as engineering, for domestic service jobs.

At a Brookings Institution conference in Washington, D.C., in January 2004, I predicted that if the pace of jobs outsourcing and occupational destruction continued, the U.S. would be a third world country in 20 years. Despite my regular updates on the poor performance of U.S. job growth in the 21st century, economists have insisted that offshoring is a manifestation of free trade and can only have positive benefits overall for Americans.

Reality has contradicted the glib economists. The new high-tech knowledge jobs are being outsourced abroad even faster than the old manufacturing jobs. Establishment economists are beginning to see the light. Writing in *Foreign Affairs*. Princeton economist and former Federal Reserve vice chairman Alan Blinder concludes that economists who insist that offshore outsourcing is merely a routine extension of international trade are overlooking a major transformation with significant consequences. Blinder estimates that 42–56 million American service sector jobs are susceptible to offshore outsourcing. Whether all these jobs leave, U.S. salaries will be forced down by the willingness of foreigners to do the work for less. . . .

Hardest-Hit Sectors

During the past five years (January 01–January 06), the information sector of the U.S. economy lost 644,000 jobs, or 17.4 per cent of its work force. Computer systems design and related work lost 105,000 jobs, or 8.5 per cent of its work force. Clearly, jobs offshoring is not creating jobs in computers and information technology. Indeed, jobs offshoring is not even creating jobs in related fields.

U.S. manufacturing lost 2.9 million jobs, almost 17 per cent of the manufacturing work force. The wipeout is across the board. Not a single manufacturing payroll classification created a single new job.

The declines in some manufacturing sectors have more in common with a country undergoing saturation bombing during war than with a "supereconomy" that is "the envy of the world." In five years, communications equipment lost 42 per cent of its work force. Semiconductors and electronic components lost 37 per cent of its work force. The work force in computers and electronic products declined 30 per cent. Electrical equipment and appliances lost 25 per cent of its employees. The work force in motor vehicles and parts declined 12 per cent. Furniture and related products lost 17 per cent of its jobs. Apparel manufacturers lost almost half of the work force. Employment in textile mills declined 43 per cent. Paper and paper products lost one-fifth of its jobs. The work force in plastics and rubber products declined by 15 per cent.

For the five-year period, U.S. job growth was limited to four areas: education and health services, state and local government, leisure and hospitality, and financial services. There was no U.S. job growth outside these four areas of domestic nontradable services. . . .

Growth Confined to Nontradables

All of the occupations with the largest projected employment growth (in terms of the number of jobs) over the next decade are in nontradable domestic services. The top ten sources of the most jobs in "superpower" America are: retail salespersons, registered nurses, postsecondary teachers, customer service representatives, janitors and cleaners, waiters and waitresses, food preparation (includes fast food), home health aides, nursing aides, orderlies and attendants, general and operations managers. Note that none of this projected employment growth will contribute one nickel toward producing goods and services that could be exported to help close the huge U.S. trade deficit. Note, also, that few of these job classifications require a college education.

Among the fastest growing occupations (in terms of rate of growth), seven of the ten are in health care and social assistance. The three remaining fields are: network systems and data analysis with 126,000 jobs projected, or 12,600 per year; computer software engineering applications with 222,000 jobs projected, or 22,200 per year; and computer software engineering systems software with 146,000 jobs projected, or 14,600 per year.

Assuming these projections are realized, how many of the computer engineering and network systems jobs will go to Americans? Not many, considering the 65,000 H-1B [foreign guest worker] visas each year (bills have been introduced in Congress to raise the number) and the loss during the past five years of 761,000 jobs in the information sector and computer systems design and related sectors.

Judging from its ten-year jobs projections, the U.S. Department of Labor does not expect to see any significant high-

Most Vulnerable U.S. Jobs

Selected occupations ranked by Princeton economist Alan Blinder as "highly offshorable":

Occupation	Number of U.S. workers
Computer programmers	389,090
Data entry keyers	296,700
Actuaries	15,770
Film and video editors	15,200
Mathematicians	2,930
Medical transcriptionists	90,380
Interpreters and translators	21,930
Economists	12,470
Graphic designers	178,530
Bookkeeping, accounting and auditing clerks	1,815,340
Microbiologists	15,250
Financial analysts	180,910

David Wessel and Bob Davis,
Wall Street Journal, *March 28, 2007.*

tech job growth in the U.S. The knowledge jobs are being outsourced even more rapidly than the manufacturing jobs. The so-called "new economy" was just another hoax perpetrated on the American people. . . .

Mistaken Analysis

The denial of jobs reality has become an art form for economists, libertarians, the Bush regime, and journalists. Except for CNN's Lou Dobbs, no accurate reporting is available in the "mainstream media."

Economists have failed to examine the incompatibility of offshoring with free trade. Economists are so accustomed to shouting down protectionists that they dismiss any complaint about globalization's impact on domestic jobs as the ignorant voice of a protectionist seeking to preserve the buggy whip industry. Matthew J. Slaughter, a Dartmouth economics professor rewarded for his service to offshoring with appointment to President Bush's Council of Economic Advisers, suffered no harm to his reputation when he wrote, "For every one job that U.S. multinationals created abroad in their foreign affiliates, they created nearly two U.S. jobs in their parent operations." In other words, Slaughter claims that offshoring is creating more American jobs than foreign ones.

How did Slaughter arrive at this conclusion? Not by consulting the [Bureau of Labor Statistics (BLS)] payroll jobs data or the BLS Occupational Employment Statistics. Instead, Slaughter measured the growth of U.S. multinational employment and failed to take into account the two reasons for the increase in multinational employment: (1) Multinationals acquired many existing smaller firms, thus raising multinational employment but not overall employment, and (2) many U.S. firms established foreign operations for the first time and thereby became multinationals, thus adding their existing employment to Slaughter's number for multinational employment. . . .

Other forms of deception are widely practiced. For example, Matthew Spiegleman, a Conference Board economist, claims that manufacturing jobs are only slightly higher paid than domestic service jobs, so there is no meaningful loss in income to Americans from offshoring. He reaches this conclusion by comparing only hourly pay and leaving out the longer manufacturing workweek and the associated benefits, such as health care and pensions.

Occasionally, however, real information escapes the spin machine. In February 2006 the National Association of Manufacturers, one of offshoring's greatest boosters, released a report, "U.S. Manufacturing Innovation at Risk," by economists Joel Popkin and Kathryn Kobe. The economists find that U.S. industry's investment in research and development [R&D] is not languishing after all. It just appears to be languishing, because it is rapidly being shifted overseas: "Funds provided for foreign-performed R&D have grown by almost 73 per cent between 1999 and 2003, with a 36 per cent increase in the number of firms funding foreign R&D."

U.S. industry is still investing in R&D after all; it is just not hiring Americans to do the research and development. U.S. manufacturers still make things, only less and less in America with American labor. U.S. manufacturers still hire engineers, only they are foreign ones, not American ones.

Polarizing Rich and Poor

In other words, everything is fine for U.S. manufacturers. It is just their former American work force that is in the doldrums. As these Americans happen to be customers for U.S. manufacturers, U.S. brand names will gradually lose their U.S. market. U.S. household median income has fallen for the past five years. Consumer demand has been kept alive by consumers' spending their savings and home equity and going deeper into debt. It is not possible for debt to forever rise faster than income.

The United States is the first country in history to destroy the prospects and living standards of its labor force. It is amazing to watch freedom-loving libertarians and free-market economists serve as apologists for the dismantling of the ladders of upward mobility that made the America of old an opportunity society.

America is seeing a widening polarization into rich and poor. The resulting political instability and social strife will be terrible.

Periodical Bibliography

The following articles have been selected to supplement the diverse views presented in this chapter.

Clive Crook   "Beyond Belief," *Atlantic Monthly*, October 2007.

Steven Greenhouse   "Offshoring Silicon Valley," *American Prospect*, June 2008.

Ron Hira   "H-1B Visas: It's Time for an Overhaul," *Business Week*, April 13, 2009.

James P. Hoffa   "Keep Mexican Trucks Out," *USA Today*, April 1, 2009.

Douglas A. Irwin   "If We Buy American, No One Else Will," *New York Times*, February 1, 2009.

Peter G. Peterson   "No Free Lunch," *National Interest*, July/August 2007.

Rachel Pulfer   "Blame America," *Canadian Business*, March 2, 2009.

Arturo Sarukhan   "Congress Doesn't Respect NAFTA," *Wall Street Journal*, March 18, 2009.

Kenneth E. Scheve and   "A New Deal for Globalization," *Foreign Affairs*,
Matthew J. Slaughter   July/August 2007.

John Snow   "Seizing Globalization's Possibilities," *Newsweek*, September 8, 2008.

Jack Welch   "A Punching Bag Named NAFTA," *Business Week*, April 28, 2008.

For Further Discussion

Chapter 1

1. In the viewpoints by Daniel T. Griswold and Michael Parenti, the authors depict globalization as an empowering force. Who does Griswold believe globalization empowers? Who does Parenti say wields the power in free trade agreements? What effect does this empowerment have on democracy in globalizing countries, according to each author? Whose argument do you find more convincing? Explain why.

2. Arun Pereira asserts that globalization is breaking down national barriers and depriving national identity of its unifying force on populations. Pereira contends that religion is stepping into the breach and helping to provide the communal glue that holds people together and gives them a sense of common identity. Do you believe Pereira's claim is accurate? Can you find real-world evidence of this happening? If not, what role do you think religion plays in an increasingly globalized world?

3. Critics of cultural globalization claim that opening more markets to American products and media sources results in an Americanization of global societies. They fear that indigenous forms of cultural expression will be overpowered by the U.S. entertainment and mercantile juggernaut. Michael Lynton, however, believes that all nations—including America—are engaged in a give-and-take relationship when it comes to cultural exchange. In addition, he provides evidence that American entertainment fare, for example, is not pushing aside native counterparts in several globalized and globalizing countries. Instead, he argues that Hollywood productions are sharing box office

receipts with local productions in those countries just as foreign films are sharing U.S. box offices. Do you believe Lynton's assessment, or do you think the modern world is simply becoming more Americanized? Explain your answer.

Chapter 2

1. After reading the viewpoints by Sherle R. Schwenninger and Peter Mandelson, decide what role you believe globalization has played in the financial crisis that stunned world markets in 2008. Do you believe that globalization's shortcomings will worsen the crisis, or do you agree with Mandelson that free trade—properly managed—can restore equilibrium to the current state of world finances? Seek opinions from other sources as well to help shape your answer.

2. Joseph E. Stiglitz maintains that the pollution inherent in the production and transportation sides of free trade can be offset by instituting a global tax on global warming emissions. Les Leopold asserts that globalization's contributions to climate change should be addressed with carbon footprint studies and reducing the distance between manufacture and market for certain products. Whose scheme do you find more appealing? Explain your reasoning by enumerating the faults and strengths of each plan.

3. Steven Weber and his colleagues contend that America's lone superpower status is a hindrance to resolving many of the problems associated with globalization. After reading this viewpoint, explain what problems the authors see with American unipolarity. Do you agree with their conclusion that the rise of another superpower will benefit American global standing? Why or why not?

Chapter 3

1. Dave Curran argues that free trade defined as the stripping away of governmental regulation can be harmful to developing nations. In his view, this form of globalization may mean that nascent industries may no longer be protected against huge conglomerates, and government support may no longer be afforded to businesses that could not otherwise thrive against multinationals. Do you believe that Curran's argument is strong, or do you believe, as Steven Horwitz contends, that open markets will always promote the public interest? Cite from both articles as you explain your answer.

2. Using what you have learned from the articles in this chapter—as well as others in the anthology—explain whether you believe globalization is benefiting low-skilled workers or leaving them behind. Be sure to quote evidence from the articles that have shaped your opinion.

3. Caroline Boin and Alec van Gelder argue that some governments in developing nations are mistakenly trying to protect their agricultural industries at the expense of feeding their hungry populations. Sophia Murphy, on the other hand, claims that forcing countries to import foods that they already produce makes them more dependent on foreign supplies and less capable of controlling the price of these commodities. Whose argument do you find more convincing? Explain why.

Chapter 4

1. John Murphy supports his claim that the North American Free Trade Agreement (NAFTA) is benefiting the three trade partners by citing statistics of continued growth in jobs and gross domestic products. Thea M. Lee offers criticism of NAFTA by proffering statistics that show a mounting trade deficit between the United States and its

two counterparts. Which argument do you find more convincing, and on what do you base your conclusion?

2. Victor A. Canto argues that outsourcing may entail the loss of some low-wage jobs for Americans, but overall the process leads to the creation of more and better jobs for U.S. workers. Ronil Hira questions this assessment, claiming that America is losing too many skilled positions to overseas competitors and generating replacement jobs mainly in low-wage markets and service professions. Using what you know from personal experience and from what you may have read on the topic, build an argument that supports one of these views.

3. In a period of economic instability—especially one that has witnessed the flight of American jobs to foreign markets—it seems reasonable, even patriotic, to support "Buy American" policies. After reading the viewpoints by Jaime Maliszewski and Gary Shapiro, do you think the American economy will benefit by supporting homegrown industry over foreign competition? Explain why, using quotes and evidence from the viewpoints.

Organizations to Contact

The editors have compiled the following list of organizations concerned with the issues debated in this book. The descriptions are derived from materials provided by the organizations. All have publications or information available for interested readers. The list was compiled on the date of publication of the present volume; the information provided here may change. Be aware that many organizations take several weeks or longer to respond to inquiries, so allow as much time as possible.

American Enterprise Institute (AEI)
1150 Seventeenth Street NW, Washington, DC 20036
(202) 862-5800 • fax: (202) 862-7177
Web site: www.aei.org

Since its founding in 1943, AEI has been working to espouse the ideas of limited government, free market economics, individual liberty and responsibility, and a strong national defense as the basis for a strong and successful United States. Generally, the institute has been supportive of globalization, seeing this trend as necessary to improving the global economy, reducing poverty, and spreading democracy. AEI's official magazine, the *American*, has published articles concerning globalization, many of which are available on the organization's Web site along with additional commentary and reports.

American Federation of Labor and Congress of Industrial Organizations (AFL-CIO)
815 Sixteenth Street NW, Washington, DC 20006
Web site: www.afl-cio.org

The AFL-CIO is a membership organization serving national and international labor unions comprising workers in varying professions including teachers, truck drivers, musicians, miners, firefighters, and farmworkers, among others. The organization's mission is to better the lives of working families by ensuring economic justice in the workplace and social justice nationwide. With regard to globalization, the AFL-CIO cautions that in many cases this trend benefits the American elite and already-wealthy corporations while placing increased economic burden on the American working class. Reports and commentary exploring the impact of globalization on the United States can be accessed online.

Cato Institute
1000 Massachusetts Ave. NW, Washington, DC   20001-5403
(202) 842-0200 • fax: (202) 842-3490
Web site: www.cato.org

The Cato Institute, a libertarian think tank, promotes public policies exemplifying the values and principles of a free market economic system coupled with limited government intervention into the private lives of American citizens. The institute insists that globalization will benefit all members of the global community by opening up markets for increased participation and profit, thereby providing opportunity for those living in poverty to advance their economic and social situations. Cato's triannual *Cato Journal* and the quarterly *Cato's Letters* are available online; in addition, the organization's Web site offers access to additional reports and commentary about the benefits of globalization.

CorpWatch
1611 Telegraph Ave., #720, Oakland, CA   94612
(510) 271-8080
Web site: www.corpwatch.org

CorpWatch works to ensure that corporations are held accountable for their actions, human rights are observed worldwide, and environmental crimes, fraud, and corruption are exposed. For CorpWatch, globalization encompasses numerous and varied subissues relating to topics such as poor labor conditions, offshoring, human rights, and international monetary policy. Fact sheets on the organization's Web site point out the gross inequalities that exist in the current global economy and provide information about the involvement, or lack thereof, of nongovernmental organizations, such as the World Bank and International Monetary Fund, in addressing these problems. Additional reports and commentary discussing the many facets of globalization can be read on the CorpWatch Web site.

Council on Foreign Relations (CFR)

The Harold Pratt House, 58 E. Sixty-eighth Street
New York, NY   10065
(212) 434-9400 • fax: (212) 434-9800
Web site: www.cfr.org

CFR is a nonpartisan think tank seeking to provide unbiased educational information on government foreign policy to its members, government officials, the media, the public, and any interested individual. The council does not endorse any single viewpoint and provides scholars an opportunity to debate current foreign policy issues. With regard to globalization, topics of interest covered by the organization range from democracy and human rights to economics to global governance. CFR's bimonthly journal, *Foreign Affairs*, publishes articles relating to these topics, and the council's Web site provides additional commentary and reports.

Economic Policy Institute (EPI)

1333 H Street NW, Suite 300, East Tower
Washington, DC   20005-4707
(202) 775-8810 • fax: (202) 775-0819
e-mail: epi@epi.org
Web site: www.epi.org

The goal of EPI is to see a prosperous and fair economy thrive in the United States. It seeks to achieve this goal by facilitating public debate about the most appropriate strategies to advance the U.S. economy and providing citizens with the tools they need to make informed decisions concerning economic policy making. The institute advocates for a new outlook on the global economy that places greater emphasis on the rights of workers. The EPI also serves as the secretariat for the Global Policy Network (GPN), a consortium of organizations from around the world dedicated to analyzing and providing suggestions to improve the state of global affairs. The official publication of the institute is the *EPI Journal*, and more information about GPN can be found at www.gpn.org.

Global Policy Forum (GPF)
777 UN Plaza, Suite 3D, New York, NY   10017
(212) 557-3161 • fax: (212) 557-3165
e-mail: gpf@globalpolicy.org
Web site: www.globalpolicy.org

GPF serves as a watchdog over policy making at the United Nations, ensuring accountability within this organization, acting as an advocate for significant international peace and justice issues, and providing citizens worldwide with the information they need to actively participate in the global society. GPF believes that security and economic justice are the keys to human development. The forum fully explores the benefits and costs of globalization and seeks to ensure that the positive impact of this trend will ultimately outweigh the negative. Reports and discussion of globalization can be read on the GPF Web site.

The Heritage Foundation
214 Massachusetts Ave. NE, Washington, DC   20002-4999
(202) 546-4400 • fax: (202) 546-8328
e-mail: info@heritage.org
Web site: www.heritage.org

A conservative public policy institute promoting policies consistent with the ideas of free enterprise, limited government, individual freedom, traditional American values, and a strong national defense, Heritage has taken a firm stance on globalization and America's role in international relations. The foundation believes that American foreign aid should be less related to monetary gifts and more focused on the promotion of democratic principles and the observance of human rights that will ultimately strengthen a country's ability to prosper. Additionally, Heritage maintains that open markets are the best way for the global economy to thrive. Heritage Web-Memos and Backgrounders providing detailed information about the organization's stance on these topics and others are accessible online.

International Forum on Globalization (IFG)

1009 General Kennedy Ave. #2, San Francisco, CA   94129
(415) 561-7650 • fax: (415) 561-7651
e-mail: ifg@ifg.org
Web site: www.ifg.org

The IFG has been working since 1994 to critique the process of globalization imposed by nongovernmental organizations such as the World Bank, the World Trade Organization, and the International Monetary Fund. The IFG worries that the development model promoted by these organizations benefits corporations and investors more than the workers and citizens of developing countries. Analysis of these organizations and their work is available on the IFG Web site.

International Monetary Fund (IMF)

700 Nineteenth Street NW, Washington, DC   20431
(202) 623-7300 • fax: (202) 623-6278
e-mail: publicaffairs@imf.org
Web site: www.imf.org

The IMF was created following World War II to promote international cooperation and trade in order to facilitate improved economic stability and the reduction of poverty worldwide. The IMF Web site provides background information on the topic of globalization as well as current information regarding the impact of the global financial crisis on the process of globalization. Additional articles examining the globalization of finance, labor, trade, and other processes can be read online.

Peterson Institute for International Economics

1750 Massachusetts Ave. NW, Washington, DC   20036-1903
(202) 328-9000 • fax: (202) 659-3225
e-mail: comments@petersoninstitute.org
Web site: www.petersoninstitute.org

Widely renowned for its neutral views, the Peterson Institute offers nonpartisan research on international economic policy. The institute addresses the issue of globalization as it relates directly to trade and jobs, but also examines the impact of globalization with regard to foreign investment in the United States, the current global financial crisis, and global warming. Policy briefs, working papers, speeches and testimony, and additional commentary on these topics and others can be read on the Peterson Institute's Web site.

Progressive Policy Institute (PPI)

600 Pennsylvania Ave. SE, Suite 400, Washington, DC   20003
(202) 547-0001 • fax: (202) 544-5014
Web site: www.ppionline.org

PPI attempts to move away from traditional views and the left-right debate to provide a progressive approach to public policy making, advocating policies that strengthen international and political freedom. The institute sees the benefit in globalization for both American workers and the global economy and encourages in-depth discussion of related issues. Commentary, testimony, and additional reports on these topics can be read online.

World Bank

1818 H Street NW, Washington, DC   20433
(202) 473-1000 • fax: (202) 477-6391
Web site: www.worldbank.org

The World Bank is a financial institution made up of two development institutions owned by 185 member countries, the International Bank for Reconstruction and Development, and the International Development Association. Together, these institutions provide financial assistance to developing countries, aiding them in improving social and financial infrastructure, such as educational systems, health care, public administration, and agricultural development and sustainability, to name a few. While acknowledging that globalization has resulted in increased inequality and environmental problems, the World Bank maintains that globalization can be a catalyst for positive change. Reports on the impact of globalization can be read on the World Bank Web site.

World Trade Organization (WTO)
Centre William Rappard, Rue de Lausanne 154
Geneva 21   CH-1211
   Switzerland
+41 22 739-5111 • fax: +41 22 731-4206
e-mail: enquiries@wto.org
Web site: www.wto.org

The WTO is an international organization providing a forum for member governments to discuss and negotiate trade agreements with the overarching goal of improving and opening global trade. The WTO sets the guidelines for the trade of goods and services, defines the protections afforded to intellectual property, and works to settle trade disputes. Detailed information about the workings of the WTO can be read online.

Bibliography of Books

Akbar Ahmed — *Journey into Islam: The Crisis of Globalization.* Washington, DC: Brookings Institution Press, 2008.

Peter Beyer and Lori Beaman — *Religion, Globalization, and Culture.* Boston: Brill, 2007.

Jagdish Bhagwati — *In Defense of Globalization.* New York: Oxford University Press, 2007.

Bill Bigelow and Bob Peterson — *Rethinking Globalization.* Milwaukee, WI: Rethinking Schools, 2002.

John Cavanagh and Jerry Mander — *Alternatives to Economic Globalization: A Better World Is Possible.* San Francisco: Berrett-Koehler, 2004.

Ha-Joon Chang — *Bad Samaritans: The Myth of Free Trade and the Secret History of Capitalism.* New York: Bloomsbury, 2008.

Michel Chossudovsky — *The Globalization of Poverty and the New World Order.* Montreal: Global Research, 2003.

Daniel Cohen — *Globalization and Its Enemies.* Cambridge, MA: MIT Press, 2007.

Lane Crothers — *Globalization and American Popular Culture.* Lanham, MD: Rowman & Littlefield, 2006.

Thomas L. Friedman — *The Lexus and the Olive Tree: Understanding Globalization.* New York: Farrar, Straus & Giroux, 2000.

Thomas L. Friedman — *The World Is Flat 3.0: A Brief History of the Twenty-first Century.* New York: Picador, 2007.

Kai Hafez — *The Myth of Media Globalization.* Cambridge, UK: Polity, 2007.

Lui F. Hebron and John F. Stack — *Globalization: Debunking the Myths.* Upper Saddle River, NJ: Prentice Hall, 2008.

David Held and Anthony McGrew — *Globalization/Anti-Globalization: Beyond the Great Divide.* Cambridge, UK: Polity, 2007.

Eric Hobsbawm — *Globalization, Democracy, and Terrorism.* London: Abacus, 2008.

Naomi Klein — *The Shock Doctrine: The Rise of Disaster Capitalism.* New York: Picador, 2008.

Frank J. Lechner and John Boli, eds. — *The Globalization Reader.* Hoboken, NJ: Wiley-Blackwell, 2007.

Barry C. Lynn — *End of the Line: The Rise and Coming Fall of the Global Corporation.* New York: Broadway, 2006.

Rebecca Todd Peters — *In Search of the Good Life: The Ethics of Globalization.* London: Continuum, 2004.

Jan Nederveen Pieterse — *Globalization and Culture: Global Melange.* Lanham, MD: Rowman & Littlefield, 2003.

John Robb and James Fallows	*Brave New War: The Next Stage of Terrorism and the End of Globalization.* Hoboken, NJ: Wiley, 2008.
Birgit Schaebler and Leif Stenberg, eds.	*Globalization and the Muslim World: Culture, Religion, and Modernity.* Syracuse, NY: Syracuse University Press, 2004.
Roger Scruton	*The West and the Rest: Globalization and the Terrorist Threat.* Wilmington, DE: Intercollegiate Studies Institute, 2003.
James Gustave Speth	*Worlds Apart: Globalization and the Environment.* Washington, DC: Island, 2003.
Joseph E. Stiglitz	*Globalization and Its Discontents.* New York: Norton, 2003.
Joseph E. Stiglitz	*Making Globalization Work.* New York: Norton, 2007.
Martin Wolf	*Why Globalization Works.* New Haven, CT: Yale University Press, 2005.

Index